THE NOVEL AS AMERICAN SOCIAL HISTORY

RICHARD LOWITT, GENERAL EDITOR

THE SKY PILOT

THE SKY PILOT

A TALE OF THE FOOTHILLS

BY

RALPH CONNOR

INTRODUCTION BY

ROBIN W. WINKS

THE UNIVERSITY PRESS OF KENTUCKY

LEXINGTON 1970

INTRODUCTION

by Robin W. Winks

At the turn of the present century Ralph Connor was one of North America's leading writers. A Canadian, he was as widely read in the United States and Great Britain as in his native country, and for many Americans the figures he had created in his first two books represented an accurate, if sentimental, picture of life in the Canadian West. In 1893 Frederick Jackson Turner had declared that the American frontier was closed, but the romance of the West remained alive and palpable on the Canadian side of the border. To Americans as well as Canadians, Connor beckoned, reinforcing the romantic conviction that Canada was the last of the Great Frontiers. As a Canadian, and as a Westerner who could embrace both sides of the border with his message, Connor was universally North American.

As with many highly successful authors, timing did much to provide Connor with his full measure of reknown. His first novel, *Black Rock: A Tale of the Selkirks,* appeared in 1898, and his second, *The Sky Pilot,* followed in 1899. Both told of life on the far western frontier. They spoke of the freedom, spiritual even more than economic, but assuredly both, that settlers might find in the high-grass country in and east of the Canadian Rockies. Both books were widely read by men who later moved into that vast region, attracted at least in part by the "velvet hills, brown or yellow or faintly green" of which the novelist wrote. Just as Joseph Altsheler would, in the 1920s, and later, draw many young men after him into a fascinated interest with the American Civil War, so would *The Sky Pilot* lead men into the paths of a muscular Christianity best practiced under "the radiant yellow light" of the West. One statistic alone goes far to explain the success of a writer now forgotten save as a historical figure, one little studied and even yet awaiting his first biographer: between 1897, when Connor submitted his first stories for publication, and 1912, shortly before he published his poorest novel, *The Patrol of the Sundance Trail*, two and a third million immigrants entered Canada. The goal of the majority was the land of the Sky Pilot.

But more than timing helped give Ralph Connor his success, his audience, and his continued relevance today. Connor saw life as a religious enterprise in which one dared all for God and for Country, shoring up the old virtues of duty, integrity, and manliness against an ever-rising surge of immigrants, many of whom he thought did not share these virtues as readily as they might. Connor was more religious in his message than were most of the other widely read romantic novelists of empire, settlement, and war in his time, but he shared many of their views. G. A. Henty wrote of wars where blood was shed while Connor wrote of wars in which souls might be saved; H. Rider Haggard would reveal how a white woman, Ayesha, could rule over black men in Africa while Connor showed how Britons (and especially Scots) served the Lord. R. M. Ballantyne, Gordon Stables, James Oliver Curwood, and many others reached out to the same market, some far more effectively than Connor could do, but none with greater sincerity or more dedication to a sense of place, purpose, and creed. Before his death Connor wrote thirty books, several of which continue to sell, and saw three million copies of his work taken up by avid readers.

By indiscriminate readers, one might also say today. For Connor's style has not worn well. Indeed, he writes badly much of the time, and one turns to him now primarily as a figure of historical interest. His cloying sentimentalism, the obviousness of his plots, the tendency to resolve difficulties by turning to coincidence, his unerring penchant for cliché, and even his efforts to achieve an authentic transcription of a variety of accents (efforts once highly praised by critics, especially in Canada), make him difficult to read with pleasure today. Yet much in his prose has survived changing tastes: his sense of humor, earthy and authentic, still rings true; his respect for the landscape, despite an inferior style which seldom could bring the Foothill Country truly alive, is ennobling in an age of environmental crises; and his respect for all men, in that he always sought the best in them and never painted a villain beyond redemption, remains at the base of Christian ethics if not doctrine. As he wrote, the Pilot helped call the Foothill Country "to a new experience." The men of that high, forlorn land had expected a preacher to bring them "chiefly pity, warning, rebuke." Instead, he gave them "respect, admiration, and open-hearted affection." In so doing, *The Sky Pilot* reached out to a continent of readers who wished to cry a bit, laugh a bit, and know that all comes right in the end. This was, after all, long before Walter van Tilburg Clark's *The Ox-Bow Incident* revealed that evil might triumph, too. In a pre-Freudian age novels that brought religion down from the pulpit sat side by side with Charles Sheldon's *In His Steps,* published in 1896, and through Connor one felt that an answer had been given to Sheldon's question, "What Would Jesus Do?"

Ralph Connor was the pseudonym of Charles William Gordon, born in Glengarry County, Canada West (present-day Ontario), in 1860. Gordon grew up in Glengarry when it was the Canadian frontier, and his best-written, if rather more parochially Canadian novel, *The Man from Glengarry,* published in 1901, drew upon this youth. Gordon's

father was a Presbyterian minister and the son was destined
for the same calling, attending the University of Toronto,
the University of Edinburgh, and Knox College. His mother
seems to have been an exceptional woman; she appeared in
virtually all of Connor's novels in an idealized form, once—
in *The Doctor* (1906)—under her own maiden name,
Margaret Robertson. Gordon was ordained in 1890 and took
up a home mission station at Banff, amidst the mountains
he would later describe as Ralph Connor. In 1894 he was
called to Winnipeg, to remain there as pastor of St. Ste-
phen's Church until he died in 1937. He served in Europe as
a chaplain to the Canadian forces during World War I,
between 1920 and 1924 was chairman of the Manitoba
Council of Industry, a board established to mediate between
capital and labor in growing Winnipeg, and in 1921 became
moderator of the Presbyterian Church. He worked to effect
the union between the Methodist and Presbyterian churches
in Canada which, in 1924, led to the creation of the United
Church of Canada, and in 1931 he visited Spain, to return
an ardent foe of fascism and a critic of Christianity for not
strongly enough opposing its rise. Until his death Gordon
remained a man of the people, himself successful and famed
in all that he did, yet mindful of that rural childhood he
described in *Glengarry School Days* (1902).

Charles William Gordon became Ralph Connor in 1897,
when he drew upon some of his mission experiences to write
three short stories for a Presbyterian journal, *The West-
minster Magazine*. These sketches of life in a British
Columbia mining camp impressed the magazine's editor,
who took the unusual step of suggesting publication as a
book. At first 1,000 copies were printed. Five thousand sold
within a few weeks, and *Black Rock* was a household word
in English-speaking Canada. Connor, having taken his
symbolic name from the standard abbreviation for the
Canadian Northwest—Can. Nor.—plunged ahead with his

second effort, *The Sky Pilot,* to show, as he said, that "it is good to be a man." Canada's West was unlike that of the United States in that law and order had preceded settlement, and the chief heroes of that law and order were corporate men, belonging to organizations such as the Hudson's Bay Company or the North West Mounted Police. There would be no shoot-outs at the O.K. corral, no Billy the Kid or Jesse James, for western Canadian fiction. But there could still be a man alone against the environment: the preacher, the man who brought God into the lives of those who needed him without knowing it, the Sky Pilot. Purposefully, didactically, Connor set out to show how God was relevant on the new frontier. *Black Rock,* noted favorably by America reviewers, sold half a million copies; its quasi-sequel, *The Sky Pilot,* published simultaneously in New York and Toronto, was even more widely reviewed, if selling slightly less, and helped make its author "comfortable," as the Victorian phrase had it. Steadily other novels followed, notably *The Prospector* (1904), *The Doctor* (1906), *The Foreigner* (1909), and *Corporal Cameron of the North West Mounted Police* (1912), rather as though Turner himself had set out to limn each of the frontier types he mentioned in his famous "thesis." Connor also wrote, as Gordon, of his experiences on the Manitoba council in *To Him That Hath* (1921), and of financial speculation in *The Arm of Gold* (1932), and he left a manuscript autobiography, *Postscript to Adventure,* which was published posthumously in 1938 with revisions by his son, J. King Gordon.

But by 1938 Ralph Connor had been forgotten, the uniform Grosset & Dunlap volumes, in green covers with garish red lettering, sitting upon shelves unread except by the historian, the student of popular literature, or the reader in search of nostalgia. Connor was remembered best for his Glengarry series, while his patriotic, religious, pluck-ridden stories seemed out of touch with the realities of a post-Passchendaele world. The Empire, the West—even God —now seemed to have acquired different meanings. Connor's obtrusive message-mongering could no longer hide the simple aesthetic fact that he did not write well; indeed, by the appearance of *The Doctor* the critics had begun to say so, and they became harsher as time passed. Further, Connor had drawn upon his experiences to the full—Hi Kendal and Bronco Bill are successfully realized in *The Sky Pilot* because they were real men—and he had little left to say. After World War I Connor slowly faded into the sunset glow which had suffused his novels.

Still, Connor remains important as one who speaks to us with the voice of those precious years at the turn of the century when all seemed right with the world. A rumble in South Africa, a splendid little war in Cuba, some trouble between Russia and the Japanese, even an aggressive America questing after Canadian reciprocity, did little between 1897 and 1912, between *Black Rock* and *Corporal Cameron,* to disturb the thought, as expressed by Ranald, then sixteen, in *The Man from Glengarry,* that "he would always be happy. What difference could anything make?"

PREFACE

The measure of a man's power to help his brother is the measure of the love in the heart of him and of the faith he has that at last the good will win. With this love that seeks not its own and this faith that grips the heart of things, he goes out to meet many fortunes, but not that of defeat.

This story is of the people of the Foothill Country; of those men of adventurous spirit, who left homes of comfort, often of luxury, because of the stirring in them to be and to do some worthy thing; and of those others who, outcast from their kind, sought to find in these valleys, remote and lonely, a spot where they could forget and be forgotten.

The waving skyline of the Foothills was the boundary of their lookout upon life. Here they dwelt safe from the scanning of the world, freed from all restraints of social law, denied the gentler influences of home and the sweet uplift of a good woman's face. What wonder if, with the new freedom beating in their hearts and ears, some rode fierce and hard the wild trail to the cut-bank of destruction!

The story is, too, of how a man with vision beyond the waving skyline came to them with firm purpose to play the brother's part, and by sheer love of them and by faith in them, win them to believe that life is priceless, and that it is good to be a man.

CONTENTS

The Sky Pilot

CHAPTER I

THE FOOTHILLS COUNTRY

Beyond the great prairies and in the shadow of
the Rockies lie the Foothills.   For nine hundred
miles the prairies spread themselves out in vast
level reaches, and then begin to climb over softly
rounded mounds that ever grow higher and sharper
till, here and there, they break into jagged points
and at last rest upon the great bases of the
mighty mountains.   These rounded hills that join
the prairies to the mountains form the Foothill
Country.   They extend for about a hundred miles
only, but no other hundred miles of the great
West are so full of interest and romance.   The
natural features of the country combine the
beauties of prairie and of mountain scenery.
There are valleys so wide that the farther side

melts into the horizon, and uplands so vast as to suggest the unbroken prairie. Nearer the mountains the valleys dip deep and ever deeper till they narrow into canyons through which mountain torrents pour their blue-gray waters from glaciers that lie glistening between the white peaks far away. Here are the great ranges on which feed herds of cattle and horses. Here are the homes of the ranchmen, in whose wild, free, lonely existence there mingles much of the tragedy and comedy, the humor and pathos, that go to make up the romance of life. Among them are to be found the most enterprising, the most daring, of the peoples of the old lands. The broken, the outcast, the disappointed, these too have found their way to the ranches among the Foothills. A country it is whose sunlit hills and shaded valleys reflect themselves in the lives of its people; for nowhere are the contrasts of light and shade more vividly seen than in the homes of the ranchmen of the Albertas.

The experiences of my life have confirmed in me the orthodox conviction that Providence sends his rain upon the evil as upon the good; else I should never have set my eyes upon the Foothill country, nor touched its strangely fascinating life,

nor come to know and love the most striking
man of all that group of striking men of the Foothill country—the dear old Pilot, as we came to call
him long afterwards. My first year in college
closed in gloom. My guardian was in despair.
From this distance of years I pity him. Then I
considered him unnecessarily concerned about
me—"a fussy old hen," as one of the boys suggested. The invitation from Jack Dale, a distant
cousin, to spend a summer with him on his ranch
in South Alberta came in the nick of time. I
was wild to go. My guardian hesitated long; but
no other solution of the problem of my disposal
offering, he finally agreed that I could not well
get into more trouble by going than by staying.
Hence it was that, in the early summer of one of
the eighties, I found myself attached to a Hudson's Bay Company freight train, making our
way from a little railway town in Montana
towards the Canadian boundary. Our train consisted of six wagons and fourteen yoke of oxen,
with three cayuses, in charge of a French half-
breed and his son, a lad of about sixteen. We
made slow enough progress, but every hour of the
long day, from the dim, gray, misty light of dawn
to the soft glow of shadowy evening, was full of

new delights to me.   On the evening of the third
day we reached the Line Stopping Place, where
Jack Dale met us.   I remember well how my
heart beat with admiration of the easy grace with
which he sailed down upon us in the loose-jointed
cowboy style, swinging his own bronco and the
little cayuse he was leading for me into the circle
of the wagons, careless of ropes and freight and
other impedimenta.   He flung himself off before
his bronco had come to a stop, and gave me a
grip that made me sure of my welcome.   It was
years since he had seen a man from home, and
the eager joy in his eyes told of long days and
nights of lonely yearning for the old days and the
old faces.   I came to understand this better after
my two years' stay among these hills that have a
strange power on some days to waken in a man
longings that make his heart grow sick.   When
supper was over we gathered about the little fire,
while Jack and the half-breed smoked and talked.
I lay on my back looking up at the pale, steady
stars in the deep blue of the cloudless sky, and
listened in fullness of contented delight to the
chat between Jack and the driver.   Now and then
I asked a question, but not too often.   It is a
listening silence that draws tales from a western

man, not vexing questions. This much I had
learned already from my three days' travel. So
I lay and listened, and the tales of that night are
mingled with the warm evening lights and the
pale stars and the thoughts of home that Jack's
coming seemed to bring.

Next morning before sun-up we had broken
camp and were ready for our fifty-mile ride.
There was a slight drizzle of rain and, though
rain and shine were alike to him, Jack insisted
that I should wear my mackintosh. This gar-
ment was quite new and had a loose cape which
rustled as I moved toward my cayuse. He was
an ugly-looking little animal, with more white in
his eye than I cared to see. Altogether, I did not
draw toward him. Nor did he to me, appar-
ently. For as I took him by the bridle he
snorted and sidled about with great swiftness,
and stood facing me with his feet planted firmly
in front of him as if prepared to reject overtures
of any kind soever. I tried to approach him with
soothing words, but he persistently backed away
until we stood looking at each other at the utmost
distance of his outstretched neck and my outstretched arm. At this point Jack came to my
assistance, got the pony by the other side of the

bridle, and held him fast till I got into position to mount. Taking a firm grip of the horn of the Mexican saddle, I threw my leg over his back. The next instant I was flying over his head. My only emotion was one of surprise, the thing was so unexpected. I had fancied myself a fair rider, having had experience of farmers' colts of divers kinds, but this was something quite new. The half-breed stood looking on, mildly interested; Jack was smiling, but the boy was grinning with delight.

"I'll take the little beast," said Jack. But the grinning boy braced me up and I replied as carelessly as my shaking voice would allow:

"Oh, I guess I'll manage him," and once more got into position. But no sooner had I got into the saddle than the pony sprang straight up into the air and lit with his back curved into a bow, his four legs gathered together and so absolutely rigid that the shock made my teeth rattle. It was my first experience of "bucking." Then the little brute went seriously to work to get rid of the rustling, flapping thing on his back. He would back steadily for some seconds, then, with two or three forward plunges, he would stop as if shot and spring straight into the upper air,

lighting with back curved and legs rigid as iron.
Then he would walk on his hind legs for a few
steps, then throw himself with amazing rapidity
to one side and again proceed to buck with vicious
diligence.

"Stick to him!" yelled Jack, through his shouts
of laughter.   "You'll make him sick before long."

I remember thinking that unless his insides
were somewhat more delicately organized than his
external appearance would lead one to suppose
the chances were that the little brute would be
the last to succumb to sickness.   To make matters
worse, a wilder jump than ordinary threw my
cape up over my head, so that I was in complete
darkness.   And now he had me at his mercy, and
he knew no pity.   He kicked and plunged and
reared and bucked, now on his front legs, now on
his hind legs, often on his knees, while I, in the
darkness, could only cling to the horn of the
saddle.   At last, in one of the gleams of light
that penetrated the folds of my enveloping cape,
I found that the horn had slipped to his side, so
the next time he came to his knees I threw myself
off.   I am anxious to make this point clear, for,
from the expression of triumph on the face of the
grinning boy, and his encomiums of the pony, I

gathered that he scored a win for the cayuse. Without pause that little brute continued for some seconds to buck and plunge even after my dismounting, as if he were some piece of mechanism that must run down before it could stop.

By this time I was sick enough and badly shaken in my nerve, but the triumphant shouts and laughter of the boy and the complacent smiles on the faces of Jack and the half-breed stirred my wrath. I tore off the cape and, having got the saddle put right, seized Jack's riding whip and, disregarding his remonstrances, sprang on my steed once more, and before he could make up his mind as to his line of action plied him so vigorously with the rawhide that he set off over the prairie at full gallop, and in a few minutes came round to the camp quite subdued, to the boy's great disappointment and to my own great surprise. Jack was highly pleased, and even the stolid face of the half-breed showed satisfaction.

"Don't think I put this up on you," Jack said. "It was that cape. He ain't used to such frills. But it was a circus," he added, going off into a fit of laughter, "worth five dollars any day."

"You bet!" said the half-breed. "Dat's make pretty beeg fun, eh?"

It seemed to me that it depended somewhat upon the point of view, but I merely agreed with him, only too glad to be so well out of the fight.

All day we followed the trail that wound along the shoulders of the round-topped hills or down their long slopes into the wide, grassy valleys. Here and there the valleys were cut through by coulées through which ran swift, blue-gray rivers, clear and icy cold, while from the hilltops we caught glimpses of little lakes covered with wild-fowl that shrieked and squawked and splashed, careless of danger. Now and then we saw what made a black spot against the green of the prairie, and Jack told me it was a rancher's shack. How remote from the great world, and how lonely it seemed!—this little black shack among these multitudinous hills.

I shall never forget the summer evening when Jack and I rode into Swan Creek. I say into— but the village was almost entirely one of imagination, in that it consisted of the Stopping Place, a long log building, a story and a half high, with stables behind, and the store in which the post-office was kept and over which the owner dwelt. But the situation was one of great beauty. On one side the prairie rambled down from the hills and then stretched away in tawny levels into the misty purple at the horizon; on the other it clambered over the round, sunny tops to the dim blue of the mountains beyond.

In this world, where it is impossible to reach absolute values, we are forced to hold things relatively, and in contrast with the long, lonely miles of our ride during the day these two houses, with their outbuildings, seemed a center of life. Some horses were tied to the rail that ran along in front of the Stopping Place.

"Hello!" said Jack, "I guess the Noble Seven are in town."

"And who are they?" I asked.

"Oh," he replied, with a shrug, "they are the *élite* of Swan Creek; and by Jove," he added, "this must be a Permit Night."

"What does that mean?" I asked, as we rode up towards the tie rail.

"Well," said Jack, in a low tone, for some men were standing about the door, "you see, this is a prohibition country, but when one of the boys feels as if he were going to have a spell of sickness he gets a permit to bring in a few gallons for medicinal purposes; and of course, the other boys being similarly exposed, he invites them to

assist him in taking preventive measures. And,"
added Jack, with a solemn wink, "it is remark-
able, in a healthy country like this, how many
epidemics come near ketching us."

And with this mystifying explanation we joined
the mysterious company of the Noble Seven.

The Company of the Noble Seven

CHAPTER II

As we were dismounting, the cries, "Hello, Jack!" "How do, Dale?" "Hello, old Smoke!" in the heartiest of tones, made me see that my cousin was a favorite with the men grouped about the door. Jack simply nodded in reply and then presented me in due form. "My tenderfoot cousin from the effete," he said, with a flourish. I was surprised at the grace of the bows made me by these roughly-dressed, wild-looking fellows. I might have been in a London drawing-room. I was put at my ease at once by the kindliness of their greeting, for, upon Jack's introduction, I was admitted at once into their circle, which, to a tenderfoot, was usually closed.

What a hardy-looking lot they were! Brown, spare, sinewy and hard as nails, they appeared like soldiers back from a hard campaign. They moved and spoke with an easy, careless air of almost lazy indifference, but their eyes had a trick

25

of looking straight out at you, cool and fearless, and you felt they were fit and ready.

That night I was initiated into the Company of the Noble Seven—but of the ceremony I regret to say I retain but an indistinct memory; for they drank as they rode, hard and long, and it was only Jack's care that got me safely home that night.

The Company of the Noble Seven was the dominant social force in the Swan Creek country. Indeed, it was the only social force Swan Creek knew. Originally consisting of seven young fellows of the best blood of Britain, "banded together for purposes of mutual improvement and social enjoyment," it had changed its character during the years, but not its name. First, its membership was extended to include "approved colonials," such as Jack Dale and "others of kindred spirit," under which head, I suppose, the two cowboys from the Ashley Ranch, Hi Kendal and "Bronco" Bill—no one knew and no one asked his other name—were admitted. Then its purposes gradually limited themselves to those of a social nature, chiefly in the line of poker-playing and whisky-drinking. Well born and delicately bred in that atmosphere of culture mingled with a sturdy common sense and a certain high chivalry which surrounds the stately homes of Britain, these young lads, freed from the restraints of custom and surrounding, soon shed all that was superficial in their make-up and stood forth in the naked simplicity of their native manhood. The West discovered and revealed the man in them, sometimes to their honor, often to their shame. The Chief of the Company was the Hon. Fred Ashley, of the Ashley Ranch, sometime of Ashley Court, England—a big, good-natured man with a magnificent physique, a good income from home, and a beautiful wife, the Lady Charlotte, daughter of a noble English family. At the Ashley Ranch the traditions of Ashley Court were preserved as far as possible. The Hon. Fred appeared at the wolf-hunts in riding-breeches and top boots, with hunting crop and English saddle, while in all the appointments of the house the customs of the English home were observed. It was characteristic, however, of western life that his two cowboys, Hi Kendal and Bronco Bill, felt themselves quite his social equals, though in the presence of his beautiful, stately wife they confessed that they "rather weakened." Ashley was a thoroughly good fellow, well up to his work as a cattle-man, and too much of a gentleman to feel, much less assert, any superiority of station. He had the largest ranch in the country and was one of the few men making money.

Ashley's chief friend, or, at least, most frequent companion, was a man whom they called "The Duke." No one knew his name, but every one said he was "the son of a lord," and certainly from his style and bearing he might be the son of almost anything that was high enough in rank. He drew "a remittance," but, as that was paid through Ashley, no one knew whence it came nor how much it was. He was a perfect picture of a man, and in all western virtues was easily first. He could rope a steer, bunch cattle, play poker or drink whisky to the admiration of his friends and the confusion of his foes, of whom he had a few; while as to "bronco busting," the virtue *par excellence* of western cattle-men, even Bronco Bill was heard to acknowledge that "he wasn't in it with the Dook, for it was his opinion that he could ride anythin' that had legs in under it, even if it was a blanked centipede." And this, coming from one who made a profession of "bronco busting," was unquestionably high praise. The Duke lived alone, except when he deigned to pay a visit to some lonely rancher who, for the marvellous charm of his talk, was delighted to have him as guest, even at the expense of the loss of a few games at poker. He made a friend of no one, though some men could tell of times when he stood between them and their last dollar, exacting only the promise that no mention should be made of his deed. He had an easy, lazy manner and a slow cynical smile that rarely left his face, and the only sign of deepening passion in him was a little broadening of his smile. Old Latour, who kept the Stopping Place, told me how once The Duke had broken into a gentle laugh. A French half-breed freighter on his way north had entered into a game of poker with The Duke, with the result that his six months' pay stood in a little heap at his enemy's left hand. The enraged freighter accused his smiling opponent of being a cheat, and was proceeding to demolish him with one mighty blow. But The Duke, still smiling, and without moving from his chair, caught the descending fist, slowly crushed the fingers open, and steadily drew the Frenchman to his knees, gripping him so cruelly in the meantime that he was forced to cry aloud in agony for mercy. Then it was that The Duke broke into a light laugh and, touching the kneeling Frenchman on his cheek with his finger-tips, said: "Look here, my man, you shouldn't play the game till you know how to do it and with whom you play." Then, handing him back the money, he added: "I want money, but not yours." Then, as he sat looking at the unfortunate wretch dividing his attention between his money and his bleeding fingers, he once more broke into a gentle laugh that was not good to hear.

The Duke was by all odds the most striking figure in the Company of the Noble Seven, and his word went farther than that of any other. His shadow was Bruce, an Edinburgh University man, metaphysical, argumentative, persistent, devoted to The Duke. Indeed, his chief ambition was to attain to The Duke's high and lordly manner; but, inasmuch as he was rather squat in figure and had an open, good-natured face and a Scotch voice of the hard and rasping kind, his attempts at imitation were not conspicuously successful. Every mail that reached Swan Creek brought him a letter from home. At first, after I had got to know him, he would give me now and then a letter to read, but as the tone became

more and more anxious he ceased to let me read
them, and I was glad enough of this. How he
could read those letters and go the pace of the
Noble Seven I could not see. Poor Bruce! He
had good impulses, a generous heart, but the
"Permit" nights and the hunts and the "round-
ups" and the poker and all the wild excesses of
the Company were more than he could stand.

Then there were the two Hill brothers, the
younger, Bertie, a fair-haired, bright-faced
youngster, none too able to look after himself,
but much inclined to follies of all degrees and
sorts. But he was warm-hearted and devoted to
his big brother, Humphrey, called "Hump," who
had taken to ranching mainly with the idea of
looking after his younger brother. And no easy
matter that was, for every one liked the lad
and in consequence helped him down.

In addition to these there were two others of
the original seven, but by force of circumstances
they were prevented from any more than a
nominal connection with the Company. Blake,
a typical wild Irishman, had joined the police at
the Fort, and Gifford had got married and, as Bill
said, "was roped tighter'n a steer."

The Noble Company, with the cowboys that

helped on the range and two or three farmers
that lived nearer the Fort, composed the settlers
of the Swan Creek country. A strange medley
of people of all ranks and nations, but while
among them there were the evil-hearted and evil-
living, still, for the Noble Company I will say
that never have I fallen in with men braver,
truer, or of warmer heart. Vices they had, all too
apparent and deadly, but they were due rather to
the circumstances of their lives than to the native
tendencies of their hearts. Throughout that
summer and the winter following I lived among
them, camping on the range with them and
sleeping in their shacks, bunching cattle in summer and hunting wolves in winter, nor did I,
for I was no wiser than they, refuse my part on
"Permit" nights; but through all not a man of
them ever failed to be true to his standard of
honor in the duties of comradeship and brotherhood.

The Coming of the Pilot

CHAPTER III

He was the first missionary ever seen in the country, and it was the Old Timer who named him. The Old Timer's advent to the Foothill country was prehistoric, and his influence was, in consequence, immense. No one ventured to disagree with him, for to disagree with the Old Timer was to write yourself down a tenderfoot, which no one, of course, cared to do. It was a misfortune which only time could repair to be a new-comer, and it was every new-comer's aim to assume with all possible speed the style and customs of the aristocratic Old Timers, and to forget as soon as possible the date of his own arrival. So it was as "The Sky Pilot," familiarly "The Pilot," that the missionary went for many a day in the Swan Creek country.

I had become schoolmaster of Swan Creek. For in the spring a kind Providence sent in the Muirs and the Bremans with housefuls of children,

35

to the ranchers' disgust, for they foresaw ploughed
fields and barbed-wire fences cramping their
unlimited ranges. A school became necessary.
A little log building was erected and I was
appointed schoolmaster. It was as schoolmaster
that I first came to touch The Pilot, for the letter
which the Hudson Bay freighters brought me
early one summer evening bore the inscription:

> *The Schoolmaster,*
>> *Public School,*
>>> *Swan Creek,*
>>>> *Alberta.*

There was altogether a fine air about the
letter; the writing was in fine, small hand, the
tone was fine, and th-re was something fine in
the signature—"Arthur Wellington Moore." He
was glad to know that there was a school and a
teacher in Swan Creek, for a school meant children, in whom his soul delighted; and in the
teacher he would find a friend, and without a
friend he could not live. He took me into his
confidence, telling me that though he had
volunteered for this far-away mission field he was
not much of a preacher and he was not at all

sure that he would succeed. But he meant to
try, and he was charmed at the prospect of having
one sympathizer at least. Would I be kind
enough to put up in some conspicuous place the
enclosed notice, filling in the blanks as I thought
best?

> *"Divine service will be held at Swan Creek*
> *in —— —— at —— o'clock.*
> *All are cordially invited.*
>
> *Arthur Wellington Moore."*

On the whole I liked his letter. I liked its
modest self-depreciation and I liked its cool
assumption of my sympathy and co-operation.
But I was perplexed. I remembered that Sunday was the day fixed for the great baseball
match, when those from "Home," as they fondly
called the land across the sea from which they
had come, were to "wipe the earth" with all
comers. Besides, "Divine service" was an
innovation in Swan Creek and I felt sure that,
like all innovations that suggested the approach
of the East, it would be by no means welcome.

However, immediately under the notice of the
"Grand Baseball Match for 'The Pain Killer' a
week from Sunday, at 2:30, Home vs. the

World," I pinned on the door of the Stopping Place the announcement:

> "*Divine service will be held at Swan Creek, in the Stopping Place Parlor, a week from Sunday, immediately upon the conclusion of the baseball match.*
> "*Arthur Wellington Moore.*"

There was a strange incongruity in the two, and an unconscious challenge as well.

All next day, which was Saturday, and, indeed, during the following week, I stood guard over my notice, enjoying the excitement it produced and the comments it called forth. It was the advance wave of the great ocean of civilization which many of them had been glad to leave behind—some could have wished forever.

To Robert Muir, one of the farmers newly arrived, the notice was a harbinger of good. It stood for progress, markets and a higher price for land; albeit he wondered "hoo he wad be keepit up." But his hard-wrought, quick-spoken little wife at his elbow "hooted" his scruples and, thinking of her growing lads, welcomed with unmixed satisfaction the coming of "the meenister." Her satisfaction was shared by all

the mothers and most of the fathers in the settlement; but by the others, and especially by that
rollicking, roistering crew, the Company of the
Noble Seven, the missionary's coming was
viewed with varying degrees of animosity.
It meant a limitation of freedom in their
wildly reckless living. The "Permit" nights
would now, to say the least, be subject to
criticism; the Sunday wolf-hunts and horse-
races, with their attendant delights, would now be
pursued under the eye of the Church, and this
would not add to the enjoyment of them. One
great charm of the country, which Bruce, himself
the son of an Edinburgh minister, and now Secre-
tary of the Noble Seven, described as "letting a
fellow do as he blanked pleased," would be gone.
None resented more bitterly than he the missionary's intrusion, which he declared to be an
attempt "to reimpose upon their freedom the
trammels of an antiquated and bigoted conven-
tionality." But the rest of the Company, while
not taking so decided a stand, were agreed that
the establishment of a church institution was an
objectionable and impertinent as well as unneces-
sary proceeding.

Of course, Hi Kendal and his friend Bronco

Bill had no opinion one way or the other. The Church could hardly affect them even remotely. A dozen years' stay in Montana had proved with sufficient clearness to them that a church was a luxury of civilization the West might well do without.

Outside the Company of the Noble Seven there was only one whose opinion had value in Swan Creek, and that was the Old Timer. The Company had sought to bring him in by making him an honorary member, but he refused to be drawn from his home far up among the hills, where he lived with his little girl Gwen and her old half-breed nurse, Ponka. The approach of the church he seemed to resent as a personal injury. It represented to him that civilization from which he had fled fifteen years ago with his wife and baby girl, and when five years later he laid his wife in the lonely grave that could be seen on the shaded knoll just fronting his cabin door, the last link to his past was broken. From all that suggested the great world beyond the run of the Prairie he shrank as one shrinks from a sudden touch upon an old wound.

"I guess I'll have to move back," he said to me gloomily.

"Why?" I said in surprise, thinking of his grazing range, which was ample for his herd.

"This blank Sky Pilot." He never swore except when unusually moved.

"Sky Pilot?" I inquired.

He nodded and silently pointed to the notice

"Oh, well, he won't hurt you, will he?"

"Can't stand it," he answered savagely, "must get away."

"What about Gwen?" I ventured, for she was the light of his eyes. "Pity to stop her studies." I was giving her weekly lessons at the old man's ranch.

"Dunno. Ain't figgered out yet about that baby." She was still his baby. "Guess she's all she wants for the Foothills, anyway. What's the use?" he added, bitterly, talking to himself after the manner of men who live much alone.

I waited for a moment, then said: "Well, I wouldn't hurry about doing anything," knowing well that the one thing an old-timer hates to do is to make any change in his mode of life. "Maybe he won't stay."

He caught at this eagerly. "That's so! There ain't much to keep him, anyway," and he rode off to his lonely ranch far up in the hills.

I looked after the swaying figure and tried to picture his past with its tragedy; then I found myself wondering how he would end and what would come to his little girl.   And I made up my mind that if the missionary were the right sort his coming might not be a bad thing for the Old Timer and perhaps for more than him.

The Pilot's Measure

CHAPTER IV

THE PILOT'S MEASURE

It was Hi Kendal that announced the arrival of the missionary. I was standing at the door of my school, watching the children ride off home on their ponies, when Hi came loping along on his bronco in the loose-jointed cowboy style.

"Well," he drawled out, bringing his bronco to a dead stop in a single bound, "he's lit."

"Lit? Where? What?" said I, looking round for an eagle or some other flying thing.

"Your blanked Sky Pilot, and he's a beauty, a pretty kid—looks too tender for this climate. Better not let him out on the range." Hi was quite disgusted, evidently.

"What's the matter with him, Hi?"

"Why, *he* ain't no parson! I don't go much on parsons, but when I calls for one I don't want no bantam chicken. No, sirree, horse I don't want no blankety-blank, pink-and-white complected

nursery kid foolin' round my graveyard. If
you're goin' to bring along a parson, why, bring
him with his eye-teeth cut and his tail feathers
on."

That Hi was deeply disappointed was quite
clear from the selection of the profanity with
which he adorned this lengthy address. It was
never the extent of his profanity, but the choice,
that indicated Hi's interest in any subject.

Altogether, the outlook for the missionary was
not encouraging. With the single exception of
the Muirs, who really counted for little, nobody
wanted him. To most of the reckless young
bloods of the Company of the Noble Seven his
presence was an offence; to others simply a nuisance, while the Old Timer regarded his advent
with something like dismay; and now Hi's
impression of his personal appearance was not
cheering.

My first sight of him did not reassure me. He
was very slight, very young, very innocent, with
a face that might do for an angel, except for the
touch of humor in it, but which seemed strangely
out of place among the rough, hard faces that
were to be seen in the Swan Creek Country. It
was not a weak face, however. The forehead

was high and square, the mouth firm, and the
eyes were luminous, of some dark color—violet, if
there is such a color in eyes—dreamy or spark-
ling, according to his mood; eyes for which a
woman might find use, but which, in a missionary's head, appeared to me one of those extraor-
dinary wastes of which Nature is sometimes guilty.

He was gazing far away into space infinitely
beyond the Foothills and the blue line of the
mountains behind them. He turned to me as I
drew near, with eyes alight and face glowing.

"It is glorious," he almost panted. "You see
this every day!" Then, recalling himself, he came
eagerly toward me, stretching out his hand.
"You are the schoolmaster, I know. Do you
know, it's a great thing? I wanted to be one, but
I never could get the boys on. They always got
me telling them tales. I was awfully disappointed. I am trying the next best thing. You
see, I won't have to keep order, but I don't think
I can preach very well. I am going to visit your
school. Have you many scholars? Do you know,
I think it's splendid? I wish I could do it."

I had intended to be somewhat stiff with him,
but his evident admiration of me made me quite
forget this laudable intention, and, as he talked

on without waiting for an answer, his enthusiasm, his deference to my opinion, his charm of manner, his beautiful face, his luminous eyes, made him perfectly irresistible; and before I was aware I was listening to his plans for working his mission with eager interest.   So eager was my interest, indeed, that before I was aware I found myself asking him to tea with me in my shack. But he declined, saying:

"I'd like to, awfully; but do you know, I think Latour expects me."

This consideration of Latour's feelings almost upset me.

"You come with me," he added, and I went.

Latour welcomed us with his grim old face wreathed in unusual smiles.   The Pilot had been talking to him, too.

"I've got it, Latour!" he cried out as he entered; "here you are," and he broke into the beautiful French-Canadian *chanson*, "Á la Claire Fontaine," to the old half-breed's almost tearful delight.

"Do you know," he went on, "I heard that first down the Mattawa," and away he went into a story of an experience with French-Canadian raftsmen, mixing up his French and English in so charming

a manner that Latour, who in his younger days
long ago had been a shantyman himself, hardly
knew whether he was standing on his head or on
his heels.

After tea I proposed a ride out to see the sunset from the nearest rising ground.   Latour, with
unexampled generosity, offered his own cayuse,
"Louis."

"I can't ride well," protested The Pilot.

"Ah! dat's good ponee, Louis," urged Latour.
"He's quiet lak wan leetle mouse; he's ride lak—
what you call?—wan horse-on-de-rock."   Under
which persuasion the pony was accepted.

That evening I saw the Swan Creek country
with new eyes—through the luminous eyes of The
Pilot.   We rode up the trail by the side of the
Swan till we came to the coulée mouth, dark and
full of mystery.

"Come on," I said, "we must get to the top
for the sunset."

He looked lingeringly into the deep shadows
and asked: "Anything live down there?"

"Coyotes and wolves and ghosts."

"Ghosts?" he asked, delightedly.   "Do you
know, I was sure there were, and I'm quite sure
I shall see them."

Then we took the Porcupine trail and climbed
for about two miles the gentle slope to the top of
the first rising ground.   There we stayed and
watched the sun take his nightly plunge into the
sea of mountains, now dimly visible.   Behind us
stretched the prairie, sweeping out level to the
sky and cut by the winding coulée of the Swan.
Great long shadows from the hills were lying
upon its yellow face, and far at the distant edge
the gray haze was deepening into purple.   Before
us lay the hills, softly curving like the shoulders
of great sleeping monsters, their tops still bright,
but the separating valleys full of shadow.   And
there, far beyond them, up against the sky, was
the line of the mountains—blue, purple, and gold,
according as the light fell upon them.   The sun
had taken his plunge, but he had left behind him
his robes of saffron and gold.   We stood long
without a word or movement, filling our hearts
with the silence and the beauty, till the gold in the
west began to grow dim.   High above all the
night was stretching her star-pierced, blue canopy,
and drawing slowly up from the east over the
prairie and over the sleeping hills the soft folds
of a purple haze.   The great silence of the dying
day had fallen upon the world and held us fast.

"Listen," he said, in a low tone, pointing to the hills. "Can't you hear them breathe?" And, looking at their curving shoulders, I fancied I could see them slowly heaving as if in heavy sleep, and I was quite sure I could hear them breathe. I was under the spell of his voice and his eyes, and nature was all living to me then.

We rode back to the Stopping Place in silence, except for a word of mine now and then which he heeded not, and, with hardly a good night, he left me at the door. I turned away feeling as if I had been in a strange country and among strange people.

How would he do with the Swan Creek folk? Could he make them see the hills breathe? Would they feel as I felt under his voice and eyes? What a curious mixture he was! I was doubtful about his first Sunday, and was surprised to find all my indifference as to his success or failure gone. It was a pity about the baseball match. I would speak to some of the men about it to-morrow.

Hi might be disappointed in his appearance, but, as I turned into my shack and thought over my last two hours with The Pilot and how he had "got" old Latour and myself, I began to think that Hi might be mistaken in his measure of The Pilot.

First Blood

CHAPTER V

One is never so enthusiastic in the early morning, when the emotions are calmest and the nerves at their steadiest. But I was determined to try to have the baseball match postponed. There could be no difficulty. One day was as much of a holiday as another to these easy-going fellows. But The Duke, when I suggested a change in the day, simply raised his eyebrows an eighth of an inch and said:

"Can't see why the day should be changed." Bruce stormed and swore all sorts of destruction upon himself if he was going to change his style of life for any man. The others followed The Duke's lead.

That Sunday was a day of incongruities. The Old and the New, the East and the West, the reverential Past and iconoclastic Present were jumbling themselves together in bewildering confusion. The baseball match was played with much vigor and profanity. The expression on The Pilot's face, as he stood watching for a while, was a curious mixture of interest, surprise, doubt and pain. He was readjusting himself. He was so made as to be extremely sensitive to his surroundings. He took on color quickly. The utter indifference to, the audacious disregard of all he had hitherto considered sacred and essential was disconcerting. They were all so dead sure. How did he know they were wrong? It was his first near view of practical, living skepticism. Skepticism in a book did not disturb him; he could put down words against it. But here it was alive, cheerful, attractive, indeed fascinating; for these men in their western garb and with their western swing had captured his imagination. He was in a fierce struggle, and in a few minutes I saw him disappear into the coulée.

Meantime the match went uproariously on to a finish, with the result that the champions of "Home" had "to stand The Painkiller," their defeat being due chiefly to the work of Hi and Bronco Bill as pitcher and catcher.

The celebration was in full swing; or as Hi put it, "the boys were takin' their pizen good an' calm," when in walked The Pilot. His face was

still troubled and his lips were drawn and blue, as
if he were in pain. A silence fell on the men as
he walked in through the crowd and up to the
bar. He stood a moment hesitating, looking
round upon the faces flushed and hot that were
now turned toward him in curious defiance. He
noticed the look, and it pulled him together.
He faced about toward old Latour and asked in a
high, clear voice:

"Is this the room you said we might have?"

The Frenchman shrugged his shoulders and
said:

"There is not any more."

The lad paused for an instant, but only for an
instant. Then, lifting a pile of hymn books he
had near him on the counter, he said in a grave,
sweet voice, and with the quiver of a smile about
his lips:

"Gentlemen, Mr. Latour has allowed me this
room for a religious service. It will give me
great pleasure if you will all join," and immediately he handed a book to Bronco Bill, who,
surprised, took it as if he did not know what to do
with it. The others followed Bronco's lead till
he came to Bruce, who refused, saying roughly:

"No! I don't want it; I've no use for it."

The missionary flushed and drew back as if he
had been struck, but immediately, as if unconsciously, The Duke, who was standing near,
stretched out his hand and said, with a courteous
bow, "I thank you; I should be glad of one."

"Thank you," replied The Pilot, simply, as he
handed him a book. The men seated themselves
upon the bench that ran round the room, or
leaned up against the counter, and most of them
took off their hats. Just then in came Muir, and
behind him his little wife.

In an instant The Duke was on his feet, and
every hat came off.

The missionary stood up at the bar, and
announced the hymn, "Jesus, Lover of My
Soul." The silence that followed was broken by
the sound of a horse galloping. A buckskin
bronco shot past the window, and in a few
moments there appeared at the door the Old
Timer. He was about to stride in when the
unusual sight of a row of men sitting solemnly
with hymn books in their hands held him fast at
the door. He gazed in an amazed, helpless way
upon the men, then at the missionary, then back
at the men, and stood speechless. Suddenly
there was a high, shrill, boyish laugh, and the

men turned to see the missionary in a fit of laughter. It certainly was a shock to any lingering ideas of religious propriety they might have about them; but the contrast between his frank, laughing face and the amazed and disgusted face of the shaggy old man in the doorway was too much for them, and one by one they gave way to roars of laughter. The Old Timer, however, kept his face unmoved, strode up to the bar and nodded to old Latour, who served him his drink, which he took at a gulp.

"Here, old man!" called out Bill, "get into the game; here's your deck," offering him his book. But the missionary was before him, and, with very beautiful grace, he handed the Old Timer a book and pointed him to a seat.

I shall never forget that service. As a religious affair it was a dead failure, but somehow I think The Pilot, as Hi approvingly said, "got in his funny work," and it was not wholly a defeat. The first hymn was sung chiefly by the missionary and Mrs. Muir, whose voice was very high, with one or two of the men softly whistling an accompaniment. The second hymn was better, and then came the Lesson, the story of the feeding of the five thousand. As the missionary finished the story, Bill, who had been listening with great interest, said:

"I say, pard, I think I'll call you just now."

"I beg your pardon!" said the startled missionary.

"You're givin' us quite a song and dance now, ain't you?"

"I don't understand." was the puzzled reply.

"How many men was there in the crowd?" asked Bill, with a judicial air.

"Five thousand."

"And how much grub?"

"Five loaves and two fishes," answered Bruce for the missionary.

"Well," drawled Bill, with the air of a man who has reached a conclusion, "that's a little too unusual for me. Why," looking pityingly at the missionary, "it ain't natarel."

"Right you are, my boy," said Bruce, with a laugh. "It's deucedly unnatural.

"Not for Him," said the missionary, quietly. Then Bruce joyfully took him up and led him on into a discussion of evidences, and from evidences into metaphysics, the origin of evil and the freedom of the will, till the missionary, as Bill said, "was rattled worse nor a rooster in the dark."

Poor little Mrs. Muir was much scandalized and looked anxiously at her husband, wishing him to take her out. But help came from an unexpected quarter, and Hi suddenly called out:

"Here you, Bill, shut your blanked jaw, and you, Bruce, give the man a chance to work off his music."

"That's so! Fair play! Go on!" were the cries that came in response to Hi's appeal.

The missionary, who was all trembling and much troubled, gave Hi a grateful look, and said:

"I'm afraid there are a great many things I don't understand, and I am not good at argument." There were shouts of "Go on! fire ahead, play the game!" but he said, "I think we will close the service with a hymn." His frankness and modesty, and his respectful, courteous manner gained the sympathy of the men, so that all joined heartily in singing, "Sun of My Soul." In the prayer that followed his voice grew steady and his nerve came back to him. The words were very simple, and the petitions were mostly for light and for strength. With a few words of remembrance of "those in our homes far away who think of us and pray for us and never forget," this strange service was brought to a close.

After the missionary had stepped out, the whole affair was discussed with great warmth. Hi Kendal thought "The Pilot didn't have no fair show," maintaining that when he was "ropin' a steer he didn't want no blanked tenderfoot to be shovin' in his rope like Bill there." But Bill steadily maintained his position that "the story of that there picnic was a little too unusual" for him. Bruce was trying meanwhile to beguile The Duke into a discussion of the physics and metaphysics of the case. But The Duke refused with quiet contempt to be drawn into a region where he felt himself a stranger. He preferred poker himself, if Bruce cared to take a hand; and so the evening went on, with the theological discussion by Hi and Bill in a judicial, friendly spirit in one corner, while the others for the most part played poker.

When the missionary returned late there were only a few left in the room, among them The Duke and Bruce, who was drinking steadily and losing money. The missionary's presence seemed to irritate him, and he played even more recklessly than usual, swearing deeply at every loss.

At the door the missionary stood looking up into the night sky and humming softly "Sun of My Soul," and after a few minutes The Duke joined in humming a bass to the air till Bruce could contain himself no longer.

"I say," he called out, "this isn't any blanked prayer-meeting, is it?"

The Duke ceased humming, and, looking at Bruce, said quietly: "Well, what is it? What's the trouble?"

"Trouble!" shouted Bruce. "I don't see what hymn-singing has to do with a poker game."

"Oh, I see! I beg pardon! Was I singing?" said The Duke. Then after a pause he added, "You're quite right. I say, Bruce, let's quit. Something has got on to your nerves." And coolly sweeping his pile into his pocket, he gave up the game. With an oath Bruce left the table, took another drink, and went unsteadily out to his horse, and soon we heard him ride away into the darkness, singing snatches of the hymn and swearing the most awful oaths.

The missionary's face was white with horror. It was all new and horrible to him.

"Will he get safely home?" he asked of The Duke.

"Don't you worry, youngster," said The Duke, in his loftiest manner, "he'll get along."

The luminous, dreamy eyes grew hard and bright as they looked The Duke in the face.

"Yes, I shall worry; but you ought to worry more."

"Ah!" said The Duke, raising his brows and smiling gently upon the bright, stern young face lifted up to his. "I didn't notice that I had asked your opinion."

"If anything should happen to him," replied the missionary, quickly, "I should consider you largely responsible."

"That would be kind," said The Duke, still smiling with his lips. But after a moment's steady look into the missionary's eyes he nodded his head twice or thrice, and, without further word, turned away.

The missionary turned eagerly to me:

"They beat me this afternoon," he cried, "but thank God, I know now they are wrong and I am right! I don't understand! I can't see my way through! But I am right! It's true! I feel it's true! Men can't live without Him, and be men!"

And long after I went to my shack that night I saw before me the eager face with the luminous eyes and heard the triumphant cry: "I feel it's true! Men can't live without Him, and be men!" and I knew that though his first Sunday ended in defeat there was victory yet awaiting him.

His Second Wind

CHAPTER VI

HIS SECOND WIND

The first weeks were not pleasant for The Pilot. He had been beaten, and the sense of failure damped his fine enthusiasm, which was one of his chief charms. The Noble Seven despised, ignored, or laughed at him, according to their mood and disposition. Bruce patronized him; and, worst of all, the Muirs pitied him. This last it was that brought him low, and I was glad of it. I find it hard to put up with a man that enjoys pity.

It was Hi Kendal that restored him, though Hi had no thought of doing so good a deed. It was in this way: A baseball match was on with The Porcupines from near the Fort. To Hi's disgust and the team's dismay Bill failed to appear. It was Hi's delight to stand up for Bill's pitching, and their battery was the glory of the Home team.

"Try The Pilot, Hi," said some one, chaffing him.

Hi looked glumly across at The Pilot standing some distance away; then called out, holding up the ball:

"Can you play the game?"

For answer Moore held up his hands for a catch. Hi tossed him the ball easily. The ball came back so quickly that Hi was hardly ready, and the jar seemed to amaze him exceedingly.

"I'll take him," he said, doubtfully, and the game began. Hi fitted on his mask, a new importation and his peculiar pride, and waited.

"How do you like them?" asked The Pilot.

"Hot!" said Hi. "I hain't got no gloves to burn."

The Pilot turned his back, swung off one foot on to the other and discharged his ball.

"Strike!" called the umpire.

"You bet!" said Hi, with emphasis, but his face was a picture of amazement and dawning delight.

Again The Pilot went through the manœuvre in his box and again the umpire called:

"Strike!'

Hi stopped the ball without holding it and set himself for the third. Once more that disconcerting swing and the whip-like action of the arm, and for the third time the umpire called:

'Strike!   Striker out!"

"That's the hole," yelled Hi.

The Porcupines were amazed. Hi looked at the ball in his hand, then at the slight figure of The Pilot.

"I say! where do you get it?"

"What?" asked Moore innocently.

"The gait!"

"The what?"

"The gait! the speed, you know!"

"Oh! I used to play in Princeton a little."

"Did, eh? What the blank blank did you quit for?"

He evidently regarded the exchange of the profession of baseball for the study of theology as a serious error in judgment, and in this opinion every inning of the game confirmed him. At the bat The Pilot did not shine, but he made up for light hitting by his base-running. He was fleet as a deer, and he knew the game thoroughly. He was keen, eager, intense in play, and before the innings were half over he was recognized as the best all-round man on the field. In the pitcher's box he puzzled the Porcupines till they grew desperate and hit wildly and blindly, amid the jeers of the spectators. The bewilderment of the Porcupines was equaled only by the enthusiasm of Hi and his nine, and when the game was over the score stood 37 to 7 in favor of the Home team.   They carried The Pilot off the field.

From that day Moore was another man.   He had won the unqualified respect of Hi Kendal and most of the others, for he could beat them at their own game and still be modest about it. Once more his enthusiasm came back and his brightness and his courage.   The Duke was not present to witness his triumph, and, besides, he rather despised the game.   Bruce was there, however, but took no part in the general acclaim; indeed, he seemed rather disgusted with Moore's sudden leap into favor.   Certainly his hostility to The Pilot and to all that he stood for was none the less open and bitter.

The hostility was more than usually marked at the service held on the Sunday following.   It was, perhaps, thrown into stronger relief by the open and delighted approval of Hi, who was prepared to back up anything The Pilot would venture to say.   Bill, who had not witnessed The Pilot's performance in the pitcher's box, but had only Hi's enthusiastic report to go upon, still preserved his judicial air.   It is fair to say, however, that there was no mean-spirited jealousy in Bill's heart even though Hi had frankly assured him that The Pilot was "a demon," and could "give him points." Bill had great confidence in Hi's opinion upon baseball, but he was not prepared to surrender his right of private judgment in matters theological, so he waited for the sermon before committing himself to any enthusiastic approval. This service was an undoubted success. The singing was hearty, and insensibly the men fell into a reverent attitude during prayer. The theme, too, was one that gave little room for skepticism. It was the story of Zaccheus, and story-telling was Moore's strong point. The thing was well done. Vivid portraitures of the outcast, shrewd, converted publican and the supercilious, self-complacent, critical Pharisee were drawn with a few deft touches. A single sentence transferred them to the Foothills and arrayed them in cowboy garb. Bill was none too sure of himself, but Hi, with delightful winks, was indicating Bruce as the Pharisee, to the latter's scornful disgust. The preacher must have noticed, for with a very clever turn the Pharisee was shown to be the kind of man who likes to fit faults upon others. Then Bill, digging his elbows into Hi's ribs, said in an audible whisper:

"Say, pardner, how does it fit now?"

"You git out!" answered Hi, indignantly, but his confidence in his interpretation of the application was shaken. When Moore came to describe the Master and His place in that ancient group, we in the Stopping Place parlor fell under the spell of his eyes and voice, and our hearts were moved within us. That great Personality was made very real and very winning. Hi was quite subdued by the story and the picture. Bill was perplexed; it was all new to him; but Bruce was mainly irritated. To him it was all old and filled with memories he hated to face. At any rate he was unusually savage that evening, drank heavily and went home late, raging and cursing at things in general and The Pilot in particular—for Moore, in a timid sort of way, had tried to quiet him and help him to his horse.

"Ornery sort o' beast now, ain't he?" said Hi, with the idea of comforting The Pilot, who stood sadly looking after Bruce disappearing in the gloom.

"No! no!" he answered, quickly, "not a beast, but a brother."

"Brother! Not much, if I know my relations!" answered Hi, disgustedly.

"The Master thinks a good deal of him," was the earnest reply.

"Git out!" said Hi, "you don't mean it! Why," he added, decidedly, "he's more stuck on himself than that mean old cuss you was tellin' about this afternoon, and without half the reason."

But Moore only said, kindly, "Don't be hard on him, Hi," and turned away, leaving Hi and Bill gravely discussing the question, with the aid of several drinks of whisky. They were still discussing when, an hour later, they, too, disappeared into the darkness that swallowed up the trail to Ashley Ranch. That was the first of many such services. The preaching was always of the simplest kind, abstract questions being avoided and the concrete in those wonderful Bible tales, dressed in modern and in western garb, set forth. Bill and Hi were more than ever his friends and champions, and the latter was heard exultantly to exclaim to Bruce:

"He ain't much to look at as a parson, but he's a-ketchin' his second wind, and 'fore long you won't see him for dust."

The Last of the Permit Sundays

CHAPTER VII

THE LAST OF THE PERMIT SUNDAYS

The spring "round-ups" were all over and Bruce had nothing to do but to loaf about the Stopping Place, drinking old Latour's bad whisky and making himself a nuisance. In vain The Pilot tried to win him with loans of books and magazines and other kindly courtesies. He would be decent for a day and then would break forth in violent argumentation against religion and all who held to it. He sorely missed The Duke, who was away south on one of his periodic journeys, of which no one knew anything or cared to ask. The Duke's presence always steadied Bruce and took the rasp out of his manners. It was rather a relief to all that he was absent from the next fortnightly service, though Moore declared he was ashamed to confess this relief.

"I can't touch him," he said to me, after the service; "he is far too clever, but," and his voice was full of pain, "I'd give something to help him."

"If he doesn't quit his nonsense," I replied, "he'll soon be past helping. He doesn't go out on his range, his few cattle wander everywhere, his shack is in a beastly state, and he himself is going to pieces, miserable fool that he is." For it did seem a shame that a fellow should so throw himself away for nothing.

"You are hard," said Moore, with his eyes upon me.

"Hard? Isn't it true?" I answered, hotly. "Then, there's his mother at home."

"Yes, but can he help it? Is it all his fault?" he replied, with his steady eyes still looking into me.

"His fault? Whose fault, then?"

"What of the Noble Seven? Have they anything to do with this?" His voice was quiet, but there was an arresting intensity in it.

"Well," I said, rather weakly, "a man ought to look after himself."

"Yes!—and his brother a little." Then he added: "What have any of you done to help him? The Duke could have pulled him up a year ago if he had been willing to deny himself a little, and so with all of you. You all do just what pleases you regardless of any other, and so you help one another down."

I could not find anything just then to say,
though afterwards many things came to me; for,
though his voice was quiet and low, his eyes were
glowing and his face was alight with the fire that
burned within, and I felt like one convicted of a
crime. This was certainly a new doctrine for
the West; an uncomfortable doctrine to practice,
interfering seriously with personal liberty, but in
The Pilot's way of viewing things difficult to
escape. There would be no end to one's responsibility. I refused to think it out.

Within a fortnight we were thinking it out with
some intentness. The Noble Seven were to have
a great "blow-out" at the Hill brothers' ranch.
The Duke had got home from his southern trip a
little more weary-looking and a little more
cynical in his smile. The "blow-out" was to be
held on Permit Sunday, the alternate to the
Preaching Sunday, which was a concession to The
Pilot, secured chiefly through the influence of Hi
and his baseball nine. It was something to have
created the situation involved in the distinction
between Preaching and Permit Sundays. Hi put
it rather graphically. "The devil takes his innin's
one Sunday and The Pilot the next," adding
emphatically, "He hain't done much scorin' yit,

but my money's on The Pilot, you bet!" Bill
was more cautious and preferred to wait developments.   And developments were rapid.

The Hill brothers' meet was unusually successful from a social point of view.   Several Permits
had been requisitioned, and whisky and beer
abounded.   Races all day and poker all night and
drinks of various brews both day and night, with
varying impromptu diversions—such as shooting
the horns off wandering steers—were the social
amenities indulged in by the noble company.
On Monday evening I rode out to the ranch,
urged by Moore, who was anxious that someone
should look after Bruce.

"I don't belong to them," he said, "you do.
They won't resent your coming."

Nor did they.   They were sitting at tea, and
welcomed me with a shout.

"Hello, old domine!" yelled Bruce, "where's
your preacher friend?"

"Where you ought to be, if you could get there
—at home," I replied, nettled at his insolent
tone.

"Strike one!" called out Hi, enthusiastically,
not approving Bruce's attitude toward his friend,
The Pilot.

"Don't be so acute," said Bruce, after the laugh had passed, "but have a drink."

He was flushed and very shaky and very noisy. The Duke, at the head of the table, looked a little harder than usual, but, though pale, was quite steady. The others were all more or less nerve-broken, and about the room were the signs of a wild night. A bench was upset, while broken bottles and crockery lay strewn about over a floor reeking with filth. The disgust on my face called forth an apology from the younger Hill, who was serving up ham and eggs as best he could to the men lounging about the table.

"It's my housemaid's afternoon out," he explained gravely.

"Gone for a walk in the park," added an.other.

"Hope *Mister* Connor will pardon the absence," sneered Bruce, in his most offensive manner.

"Don't mind him," said Hi, under his breath, "the blue devils are runnin' him down."

This became more evident as the evening went on. From hilarity Bruce passed to sullen ferocity, with spasms of nervous terror. Hi's attempts to soothe him finally drove him mad, and he drew his revolver, declaring he could look after himself, in proof of which he began to shoot out the lights.

The men scrambled into safe corners, all but The Duke, who stood quietly by watching Bruce shoot. Then saying:

"Let me have a try, Bruce," he reached across and caught his hand.

"No! you don't," said Bruce, struggling. "No man gets my gun."

He tore madly at the gripping hand with both of his, but in vain, calling out with frightful oaths:

"Let go! let go! I'll kill you! I'll kill you!"

With a furious effort he hurled himself back from the table, dragging The Duke partly across. There was a flash and a report and Bruce collapsed, The Duke still gripping him. When they lifted him up he was found to have an ugly wound in his arm, the bullet having passed through the fleshy part. I bound it up as best I could and tried to persuade him to go to bed. But he would go home. Nothing could stop him. Finally The Duke agreed to go with him, and off they set, Bruce loudly protesting that he could get home alone and did not want anyone.

It was a dismal break-up to the meet, and we all went home feeling rather sick, so that it gave me no pleasure to find Moore waiting in my shack for my report of Bruce. It was quite vain for me to make light of the accident to him. His eyes were wide open with anxious fear when I had done.

"You needn't tell me not to be anxious," he said, "you are anxious yourself. I see it, I feel it."

"Well, there's no use trying to keep things from you," I replied, "but I am only a little anxious. Don't you go beyond me and work yourself up into a fever over it."

"No," he answered quietly, "but I wish his mother were nearer."

"Oh, bosh, it isn't coming to that; but I wish he were in better shape. He is broken up badly without this hole in him."

He would not leave till I had promised to take him up the next day, though I was doubtful enough of his reception. But next day The Duke came down, his black bronco, Jingo, wet with hard riding.

"Better come up, Connor," he said, gravely, "and bring your bromides along. He has had a bad night and morning and fell asleep only before I came away. I expect he'll wake in delirium. It's the whisky more than the bullet. Snakes, you know."

In ten minutes we three were on the trail, for Moore, though not invited, quietly announced his intention to go with us.

"Oh, all right," said The Duke, indifferently, "he probably won't recognize you any way."

We rode hard for half an hour till we came within sight of Bruce's shack, which was set back into a little poplar bluff.

"Hold up!" said The Duke. "Was that a shot?" We stood listening. A rifle-shot rang out, and we rode hard. Again The Duke halted us, and there came from the shack the sound of singing. It was an old Scotch tune.

"The twenty-third Psalm," said Moore, in a low voice.

We rode into the bluff, tied up our horses and crept to the back of the shack. Looking through a crack between the logs, I saw a gruesome thing. Bruce was sitting up in bed with a Winchester rifle across his knees and a belt of cartridges hanging over the post. His bandages were torn off, the blood from his wound was smeared over his bare arms and his pale. ghastly face; his eyes

were wild with mad terror, and he was shouting
at the top of his voice the words:

"The Lord's my shepherd, I'll not want,
   He makes me down to lie
In pastures green, He leadeth me
   The quiet waters by."

Now and then he would stop to say in an awe-
some whisper, "Come out here, you little devils!"
and bang would go his rifle at the stovepipe,
which was riddled with holes. Then once more
in a loud voice he would hurry to begin the Psalm,

"The Lord's my Shepherd."

Nothing that my memory brings to me makes
me chill like that picture—the low log shack,
now in cheerless disorder; the ghastly object
upon the bed in the corner, with blood-smeared
face and arms and mad terror in the eyes; the
awful cursings and more awful psalm-singing,
punctuated by the quick report of the deadly rifle.

For some moments we stood gazing at one
another; then The Duke said, in a low, fierce
tone, more to himself than to us:

"This is the last. There'll be no more of this
cursed folly among the boys."

And I thought it a wise thing in The Pilot that
he answered not a word.

The Pilot's Grip

The Canyon Flowers

CHAPTER XIII

THE CANYON FLOWERS

The Pilot's first visit to Gwen had been a
triumph. But none knew better than he that the
fight was still to come, for deep in Gwen's heart
were thoughts whose pain made her forget all
other.

"Was it God let me fall?" she asked abruptly
one day, and The Pilot knew the fight was on;
but he only answered, looking fearlessly into her
eyes:

"Yes, Gwen dear."

"Why did He let me fall?" and her voice was
very deliberate.

"I don't know, Gwen dear," said The Pilot
steadily. "He knows."

"And does He know I shall never ride again?
Does He know how long the days are, and the
nights when I can't sleep? Does He know?"

"Yes, Gwen dear," said The Pilot, and the
tears were standing in his eyes, though his voice
was still steady enough.

"Are you sure He knows?" The voice was painfully intense.

"Listen to me, Gwen," began The Pilot, in great distress, but she cut him short.

"Are you quite sure He knows? Answer me!" she cried, with her old imperiousness.

"Yes, Gwen, He knows all about you."

"Then what do you think of Him, just because He's big and strong, treating a little girl that way?" Then she added, viciously: "I hate Him! I don't care! I hate Him!"

But The Pilot did not wince. I wondered how he would solve that problem that was puzzling, not only Gwen, but her father and The Duke, and all of us—the *why* of human pain.

"Gwen," said The Pilot, as if changing the subject, "did it hurt to put on the plaster jacket?"

"You just bet!" said Gwen, lapsing in her English, as The Duke was not present; "it was worse than anything—awful! They had to straighten me out, you know," and she shuddered at the memory of that pain.

"What a pity your father or The Duke was not here!" said The Pilot, earnestly.

"Why, they were both here!"

"What a cruel shame!" burst out The Pilot. "Don't they care for you any more?"

"Of course they do," said Gwen, indignantly.

"Why didn't they stop the doctors from hurting you so cruelly?"

"Why, they let the doctors. It is going to help me to sit up and perhaps to walk about a little," answered Gwen, with blue-gray eyes open wide.

"Oh," said The Pilot, "it was very mean to stand by and see you hurt like that."

"Why, you silly," replied Gwen, impatiently, "they want my back to get straight and strong."

"Oh, then they didn't do it just for fun or for nothing?" said The Pilot, innocently.

Gwen gazed at him in amazed and speechless wrath, and he went on:

"I mean they love you though they let you be hurt; or rather they let the doctors hurt you *because* they loved you and wanted to make you better."

Gwen kept her eyes fixed with curious earnestness upon his face till the light began to dawn.

"Do you mean," she began slowly, "that though God let me fall, He loves me?"

The Pilot nodded; he could not trust his voice.

"I wonder if that can be true," she said, as if

to herself; and soon we said good-by and came away—The Pilot, limp and voiceless, but I triumphant, for I began to see a little light for Gwen.

But the fight was by no means over; indeed, it was hardly well begun. For when the autumn came, with its misty, purple days, most glorious of all days in the cattle country, the old restlessness came back and the fierce refusal of her lot. Then came the day of the round-up. Why should she have to stay while all went after the cattle? The Duke would have remained, but she impatiently sent him away. She was weary and heart-sick, and, worst of all, she began to feel that most terrible of burdens, the burden of her life to others. I was much relieved when The Pilot came in fresh and bright, waving a bunch of wild-flowers in his hand.

"I thought they were all gone," he cried. "Where do you think I found them? Right down by the big elm root," and, though he saw by the settled gloom of her face that the storm was coming, he went bravely on picturing the canyon in all the splendor of its autumn dress. But the spell would not work. Her heart was out on the sloping hills, where the cattle were bunching and crowding with tossing heads and rattling horns, and it was in a voice very bitter and impatient that she cried:

"Oh, I am sick of all this! I want to ride! I want to see the cattle and the men and—and— and all the things outside." The Pilot was cowboy enough to know the longing that tugged at her heart for one wild race after the calves or steers, but he could only say:

"Wait, Gwen. Try to be patient."

"I am patient; at least I have been patient for two whole months, and it's no use, and I don't believe God cares one bit!"

"Yes, He does, Gwen, more than any of us," replied The Pilot, earnestly.

"No, He does not care," she answered, with angry emphasis, and The Pilot made no reply.

"Perhaps," she went on, hesitatingly, "He's angry because I said I didn't care for Him, you remember? That was very wicked. But don't you think I'm punished nearly enough now? You made me very angry, and I didn't really mean it."

Poor Gwen! God had grown to be very real to her during these weeks of pain, and very terrible. The Pilot looked down a moment into the blue-gray eyes, grown so big and so pitiful, and hurriedly dropping on his knees beside the bed he said, in a very unsteady voice:

"Oh, Gwen, Gwen, He's not like that. Don't you remember how Jesus was with the poor sick people? That's what He's like."

"Could Jesus make me well?"

"Yes, Gwen."

"Then why doesn't He?" she asked; and there was no impatience now, but only trembling anxiety as she went on in a timid voice: "I asked Him to, over and over, and said I would wait two months, and now it's more than three. Are you quite sure He hears now?" She raised herself on her elbow and gazed searchingly into The Pilot's face. I was glad it was not into mine. As she uttered the words, "Are you quite sure?" one felt that things were in the balance. I could not help looking at The Pilot with intense anxiety. What would he answer? The Pilot gazed out of the window upon the hills for a few moments. How long the silence seemed! Then, turning, looked into the eyes that searched his so steadily and answered simply:

"Yes, Gwen, I am quite sure!" Then, with quick inspiration, he got her mother's Bible and said: "Now, Gwen, try to see it as I read." But, before he read, with the true artist's instinct he created the proper atmosphere. By a few vivid words he made us feel the pathetic loneliness of the Man of Sorrows in His last sad days. Then he read that masterpiece of all tragic picturing, the story of Gethsemane. And as he read we saw it all. The garden and the trees and the sorrow-stricken Man alone with His mysterious agony. We heard the prayer so pathetically submissive and then, for answer, the rabble and the traitor.

Gwen was far too quick to need explanation, and The Pilot only said, "You see, Gwen, God gave nothing but the best—to His own Son only the best."

"The best? They took Him away, didn't they?" She knew the story well.

"Yes, but listen." He turned the leaves rapidly and read: " 'We see Jesus for the suffering of death crowned with glory and honor.' That is how He got His Kingdom."

Gwen listened silent but unconvinced, and then said slowly:

"But how can this be best for me? I am no use to anyone. It can't be best to just lie here and make them all wait on me, and—and—I did want to help daddy—and—oh—I know they will get tired of me! They are getting tired already—I—I—can't help being hateful.''

She was by this time sobbing as I had never heard her before—deep, passionate sobs. Then again the Pilot had an inspiration.

"Now, Gwen," he said severely, "you know we're not as mean as that, and that you are just talking nonsense, every word. Now I'm going to smooth out your red hair and tell you a story.''

"It's *not* red," she cried, between her sobs. This was her sore point.

"It is red, as red can be; a beautiful, shining purple *red*," said The Pilot emphatically, beginning to brush.

"Purple!" cried Gwen, scornfully.

"Yes, I've seen it in the sun, purple. Haven't you?" said The Pilot, appealing to me. "And my story is about the canyon, our canyon, your canyon, down there.''

"Is it true?" asked Gwen, already soothed by the cool, quick-moving hands.

"True? It's as true as—as—" he glanced round the room, "as the Pilgrim's Progress." This was satisfactory, and the story went on.

"At first there were no canyons, but only the broad, open prairie. One day the Master of the Prairie, walking out over his great lawns, where were only grasses, asked the Prairie, 'Where are your flowers?' and the Prairie said, 'Master, I have no seeds.' Then he spoke to the birds, and they carried seeds of every kind of flower and strewed them far and wide, and soon the Prairie bloomed with crocuses and roses and buffalo beans and the yellow crowfoot and the wild sunflowers and the red lilies all the summer long. Then the Master came and was well pleased; but he missed the flowers he loved best of all, and he said to the Prairie: 'Where are the clematis and the columbine, the sweet violets and wind flowers, and all the ferns and flowering shrubs?' And again he spoke to the birds, and again they carried all the seeds and strewed them far and wide. But, again, when the Master came, he could not find the flowers he loved best of all, and he said: 'Where are those, my sweetest flowers?' and the Prairie cried sorrowfully: 'Oh, Master, I cannot keep the flowers, for the winds sweep fiercely, and the sun beats upon my breast, and they wither up and fly away.' Then the Master spoke to the Lightning, and with one swift blow the Lightning cleft the Prairie to the heart. And the Prairie rocked and groaned in agony, and for many a day moaned bitterly over its black, jagged, gaping wound. But the Little Swan poured its waters through the cleft, and carried down deep black mould, and once more the birds carried seeds and strewed them in the canyon. And after a long time the rough rocks were decked out with soft mosses and trailing vines, and all the nooks were hung with clematis and columbine, and great elms lifted their huge tops high up into the sunlight, and down about their feet clustered the low cedars and balsams, and everywhere the violets and wind-flower and maiden-hair grew and bloomed, till the canyon became the Master's place for rest and peace and joy."

The quaint tale was ended, and Gwen lay quiet for some moments, then said gently:

"Yes! The canyon flowers are much the best Tell me what it means."

Then The Pilot read to her: "The fruits—I'll read 'flowers'—of the Spirit are love, joy, peace, long-suffering, gentleness, goodness, faith, meekness, self-control, and some of these grow only in the canyon."

"Which are the canyon flowers?" asked Gwen softly, and The Pilot answered:

"Gentleness, meekness, self-control; but though the others, love, joy, peace, bloom in the open, yet never with so rich a bloom and so sweet a perfume as in the canyon."

For a long time Gwen lay quite still, and then said wistfully, while her lip trembled:

"There are no flowers in my canyon, but only ragged rocks."

"Some day they will bloom, Gwen dear; He will find them, and we, too, shall see them."

Then he said good-by and took me away. He had done his work that day.

We rode through the big gate, down the sloping hill, past the smiling, twinkling little lake, and down again out of the broad sunshine into the shadows and soft lights of the canyon. As we followed the trail that wound among the elms and cedars, the very air was full of gentle stillness; and as we moved we seemed to feel the touch of loving hands that lingered while they left us, and every flower and tree and vine and shrub and the soft mosses and the deep-bedded ferns whispered, as we passed, of love and peace and joy.

To The Duke it was all a wonder, for as the

days shortened outside they brightened inside;
and every day, and more and more Gwen's room
became the brightest spot in all the house, and
when he asked The Pilot:

"What did you do to the Little Princess, and
what's all this about the canyon and its flowers?"
The Pilot said, looking wistfully into The Duke's
eyes:

"The fruits of the Spirit are love, peace, long-
suffering, gentleness, goodness, faith, meekness,
self-control, and some of these are found only in
the canyon," and The Duke, standing up straight,
handsome and strong, looked back at The Pilot
and said, putting out his hand:

"Do you know, I believe you're right."

"Yes, I'm quite sure," answered The Pilot,
simply.   Then, holding The Duke's hand as
long as one man dare hold another's, he added:
"When you come to your canyon, remember."

"When I come!" said The Duke, and a quick
spasm of pain passed over his handsome face—
"God help me, it's not too far away now."   Then
he smiled again his old, sweet smile, and said:

"Yes, you are all right, for, of all flowers I
have seen, none are fairer or sweeter than those
that are waving in Gwen's Canyon."

Bill's Bluff

CHAPTER XIV

BILL'S BLUFF

The Pilot had set his heart upon the building of a church in the Swan Creek district, partly because he was human and wished to set a mark of remembrance upon the country, but more because he held the sensible opinion that a congregation, as a man, must have a home if it is to stay.

All through the summer he kept setting this as an object at once desirable and possible to achieve. But few were found to agree with him.

Little Mrs. Muir was of the few, and she was not to be despised, but her influence was neutralized by the solid immobility of her husband. He had never done anything sudden in his life. Every resolve was the result of a long process of mind, and every act of importance had to be previewed from all possible points. An honest man, strongly religious, and a great admirer of The Pilot, but slow-moving as a glacier, although with plenty of fire in him deep down.

"He's soond at the hairt, ma man Robbie," his wife said to The Pilot, who was fuming and fretting at the blocking of his plans, "but he's terrible deleeberate. Bide ye a bit, laddie. He'll come tae."

"But meantime the summer's going and nothing will be done," was The Pilot's distressed and impatient answer.

So a meeting was called to discuss the question of building a church, with the result that the five men and three women present decided that for the present nothing could be done. This was really Robbie's opinion, though he refused to do or say anything but grunt, as The Pilot said to me afterwards, in a rage. It is true, Williams, the storekeeper just come from "across the line," did all the talking, but no one paid much attention to his fluent fatuities except as they represented the unexpressed mind of the dour, exasperating little Scotchman, who sat silent but for an "ay" now and then, so expressive and conclusive that everyone knew what he meant, and that discussion was at an end. The schoolhouse was quite sufficient for the present; the people were too few and too poor and they were getting on well under the leadership of their present minister. These were the arguments which Robbie's "ay" stamped as quite unanswerable.

It was a sore blow to The Pilot, who had set his heart upon a church, and neither Mrs. Muir's "hoots" at her husband's slowness nor her promises that she "wad mak him hear it" could bring comfort or relieve his gloom.

In this state of mind he rode up with me to pay our weekly visit to the little girl shut up in her lonely house among the hills.

It had become The Pilot's custom during these weeks to turn for cheer to that little room, and seldom was he disappointed. She was so bright, so brave, so cheery, and so full of fun, that gloom faded from her presence as mist before the sun, and impatience was shamed into content.

Gwen's bright face—it was almost always bright now—and her bright welcome did something for The Pilot, but the feeling of failure was upon him, and failure to his enthusiastic nature was worse than pain. Not that he confessed either to failure or gloom; he was far too true a man for that; but Gwen felt his depression in spite of all his brave attempts at brightness, and insisted that he was ill, appealing to me.

"Oh, it's only his church," I said, proceeding

to give her an account of Robbie Muir's silent, solid inertness, and how he had blocked The Pilot's scheme.

"What a shame!" cried Gwen, indignantly. "What a bad man he must be!"

The Pilot smiled. "No, indeed," he answered; "why, he's the best man in the place, but I wish he would say or do something. If he would only get mad and swear I think I should feel happier."

Gwen looked quite mystified.

"You see, he sits there in solemn silence looking so tremendously wise that most men feel foolish if they speak, while as for doing anything the idea appears preposterous, in the face of his immovableness."

"I can't bear him!" cried Gwen. "I should like to stick pins in him."

"I wish some one would," answered The Pilot. "It would make him seem more human if he could be made to jump."

"Try again," said Gwen, "and get someone to make him jump."

"It would be easier to build the church," said The Pilot, gloomily.

"I could make him jump," said Gwen, viciously, "and I *will*," she added, after a pause.

"You!" answered The Pilot, opening his eyes. "How?"

"I'll find some way," she replied, resolutely.

And so she did, for when the next meeting was called to consult as to the building of a church, the congregation, chiefly of farmers and their wives, with Williams, the storekeeper, were greatly surprised to see Bronco Bill, Hi, and half a dozen ranchers and cowboys walk in at intervals and solemnly seat themselves. Robbie looked at them with surprise and a little suspicion. In church matters he had no dealings with the Samaritans from the hills, and while, in their unregenerate condition, they might be regarded as suitable objects of missionary effort, as to their having any part in the direction, much less control, of the church policy—from such a notion Robbie was delivered by his loyal adherence to the scriptural injunction that he should not cast pearls before swine.

The Pilot, though surprised to see Bill and the cattle men, was none the less delighted, and faced the meeting with more confidence. He stated the question for discussion: Should a church building be erected this summer in Swan Creek? and he put his case well. He showed the

need of a church for the sake of the congregation, for the sake of the men in the district, the
families growing up, the incoming settlers, and
for the sake of the country and its future. He
called upon all who loved their church and their
country to unite in this effort. It was an enthusiastic appeal and all the women and some of the
men were at once upon his side.

Then followed dead, solemn silence. Robbie
was content to wait till the effect of the speech
should be dissipated in smaller talk. Then he
gravely said:

"The kirk wad be a gran' thing, nae doot, an'
they wad a' dootless"—with a suspicious glance
toward Bill—"rejoice in its erection. But we
maun be cautious, an' I wad like to enquire hoo
much money a kirk cud be built for, and whaur
the money wad come frae?"

The Pilot was ready with his answer. The
cost would be $1,200. The Church Building
Fund would contribute $200, the people could give
$300 in labor, and the remaining $700 he thought
could be raised in the district in two years' time.

"Ay," said Robbie, and the tone and manner
were sufficient to drench any enthusiasm with the
chilliest of water. So much was this the case

that the chairman, Williams, seemed quite justified in saying:

"It is quite evident that the opinion of the meeting is adverse to any attempt to load the community with a debt of one thousand dollars," and he proceeded with a very complete statement of the many and various objections to any attempt at building a church this year. The people were very few, they were dispersed over a large area, they were not interested sufficiently, they were all spending money and making little in return; he supposed, therefore, that the meeting might adjourn.

Robbie sat silent and expressionless in spite of his little wife's anxious whispers and nudges. The Pilot looked the picture of woe, and was on the point of bursting forth, when the meeting was startled by Bill.

"Say, boys! they hain't much stuck on their shop, heh?" The low, drawling voice was perfectly distinct and arresting.

"Hain't got no use for it, seemingly," was the answer from the dark corner.

"Old Scotchie takes his religion out in prayin', I guess," drawled in Bill, "but wants to sponge for his plant."

This reference to Robbie's proposal to use the school moved the youngsters to tittering and made the little Scotchman squirm, for he prided himself upon his independence.

"There ain't $700 in the hull blanked outfit." This was a stranger's voice, and again Robbie squirmed, for he rather prided himself also on his ability to pay his way.

"No good!" said another emphatic voice. "A blanked lot o' psalm-singing snipes."

"Order, order!" cried the chairman.

"Old Windbag there don't see any show for swipin' the collection, with Scotchie round," said Hi, with a following ripple of quiet laughter, for Williams' reputation was none too secure.

Robbie was in a most uncomfortable state of mind. So unusually stirred was he that for the first time in his history he made a motion.

"I move we adjourn, Mr Chairman." he said, in a voice which actually vibrated with emotion.

"Different here! eh, boys?" drawled Bill.

"You bet," said Hi, in huge delight. "The meetin' ain't out yit."

"Ye can bide till mor-r-nin'," said Robbie, angrily. "A'm gaen hame," beginning to put on his coat.

"Seems as if he orter give the password," drawled Bill.

"Right you are, pardner," said Hi, springing to the door and waiting in delighted expectation for his friend's lead.

Robbie looked at the door, then at his wife, hesitated a moment, I have no doubt wishing her home. Then Bill stood up and began to speak.

"Mr. Chairman, I hain't been called on for any remarks——"

"Go on!" yelled his friends from the dark corner. "Hear! hear!"

"An' I didn't feel as if this war hardly my game, though The Pilot ain't mean about invitin' a feller on Sunday afternoons. But them as runs the shop don't seem to want us fellers round too much."

Robbie was gazing keenly at Bill, and here shook his head, muttering angrily: "Hoots, nonsense! ye're welcome eneuch."

"But," went on Bill, slowly, "I guess I've been on the wrong track. I've been a-cherishin' the opinion" ["Hear! hear!" yelled his admirers], "cherishin' the opinion," repeated Bill, "that these fellers," pointing to Robbie, "was stuck on religion, which I ain't much myself, and reely

consarned about the blocking ov the devil, which
The Pilot says can't be did without a regular
Gospel factory.   O' course, it tain't any biznis ov
mine, but if us fellers was reely only sot on anything condoocin'," ["Hear! hear!" yelled Hi, in
ecstasy], "condoocin'," repeated Bill slowly and
with relish, "to the good ov the Order" (Bill was
a brotherhood man), "I b'lieve I know whar five
hundred dollars mebbe cud per'aps be got."

"You bet your sox," yelled the strange voice,
in chorus with other shouts of approval.

"O' course, I ain't no bettin' man," went on
Bill, insinuatingly, "as a regular thing, but I'd
gamble a few jist here on this pint; if the boys
was stuck on anythin' costin' about seven hundred dollars, it seems to me likely they'd git it in
about two days, per'aps."

Here Robbie grunted out an "ay" of such ful-
ness of contemptuous unbelief that Bill paused,
and, looking over Robbie's head, he drawled out,
even more slowly and mildly:

"I ain't much given to bettin', as I remarked
before, but, if a man shakes money at me on that
proposition, I'd accommodate him to a limited
extent." ["Hear! hear! Bully boy!" yelled Hi
again, from the door.] "Not bein' too bold, I

cherish the opinion" [again yells of approval
from the corner], "that even for this here Gospel
plant, seein' The Pilot's rather sot onto it, I
b'lieve the boys could find five hundred dollars
inside ov a month, if perhaps these fellers cud
wiggle the rest out ov their pants."

Then Robbie was in great wrath and, stung by
the taunting, drawling voice beyond all self-com-
mand, he broke out suddenly:

"Ye'll no can mak that guid, I doot."

"D'ye mean I ain't prepared to back it up?"

"Ay," said Robbie, grimly.

" 'Tain't likely I'll be called on; I guess $500
is safe enough," drawled Bill, cunningly drawing
him on.   Then Robbie bit.

"Oo ay!" said he, in a voice of quiet contempt,
"the twa hunner wull be here and 'twull wait ye
long eneuch, I'se warrant ye."

Then Bill nailed him.

"I hain't got my card case on my person," he
said, with a slight grin.

"Left it on the pianner," suggested Hi, who
was in a state of great hilarity at Bill's success in
drawing the Scottie.

"But," Bill proceeded, recovering himself, and
with increasing suavity, "if some gentleman would

mark down the date of the almanac I cherish the opinion" [cheers from the corner] "that in one month from to-day there will be five hundred dollars lookin' round for two hundred on that there desk mebbe, or p'raps you would incline to two fifty," he drawled, in his most winning tone to Robbie, who was growing more impatient every moment.

"Nae matter tae me. Ye're haverin' like a daft loon, ony way."

"You will make a memento of this slight transaction, boys, and per'aps the schoolmaster will write it down," said Bill.

It was all carefully taken down, and amid much enthusiastic confusion the ranchers and their gang carried Bill off to Old Latour's to "licker up," while Robbie, in deep wrath but in dour silence, went off through the dark with his little wife following some paces behind him. His chief grievance, however, was against the chairman for "allooin' sic a disorderly pack o' loons tae disturb respectable fowk," for he could not hide the fact that he had been made to break through his accustomed defence line of immovable silence. I suggested, conversing with him next day upon the matter, that Bill was probably only chaffing.

"Ay," said Robbie, in great disgust, "the daft eejut, he wad mak a fule o' onything or ony-buddie."

That was the sorest point with poor Robbie. Bill had not only cast doubts upon his religious sincerity, which the little man could not endure, but he had also held him up to the ridicule of the community, which was painful to his pride. But when he understood, some days later, that Bill was taking steps to back up his offer and had been heard to declare that "he'd make them pious ducks take water if he had to put up a year's pay," Robbie went quietly to work to make good his part of the bargain. For his Scotch pride would not suffer him to refuse a challenge from such a quarter.

Bill's Partner

CHAPTER XV

The next day everyone was talking of Bill's bluffing the church people, and there was much quiet chuckling over the discomfiture of Robbie Muir and his party.

The Pilot was equally distressed and bewildered, for Bill's conduct, so very unusual, had only one explanation—the usual one for any folly in that country.

"I wish he had waited till after the meeting to go to Latour's. He spoiled the last chance I had. There's no use now," he said, sadly.

"But he may do something," I suggested.

"Oh, fiddle!" said The Pilot, contemptuously. "He was only giving Muir 'a song and dance,' as he would say. The whole thing is off."

But when I told Gwen the story of the night's proceedings, she went into raptures over Bill's grave speech and his success in drawing the canny Scotchman.

"Oh, lovely! Dear old Bill and his 'cherished

opinion.' Isn't he just lovely? Now he'll do something.

"Who, Bill?"

"No, that stupid Scottie." This was her name for the immovable Robbie.

"Not he, I'm afraid. Of course Bill was just bluffing him. But it was good sport."

"Oh, lovely! I knew he'd do something."

"Who? Scottie?" I asked, for her pronouns were perplexing.

"No!" she cried, "Bill! He promised he would, you know," she added.

"So you were at the bottom of it?" I said, amazed.

"Oh, dear! Oh, dear!" she kept crying, shrieking with laughter over Bill's cherishing opinions and desires. "I shall be ill. Dear old Bill. He said he'd 'try to get a move on to him.'"

Before I left that day, Bill himself came to the Old Timer's ranch, inquiring in a casual way "if the 'boss' was in."

"Oh, Bill!" called out Gwen, "come in here at once; I want you."

After some delay and some shuffling with hat and spurs, Bill lounged in and set his lank form upon the extreme end of a bench at the door, try-

ing to look unconcerned as he remarked: "Gittin'
cold. Shouldn't wonder if we'd have a little
snow."

"Oh, come here," cried Gwen, impatiently,
holding out her hand. "Come here and shake
hands."

Bill hesitated, spat out into the other room his
quid of tobacco, and swayed awkwardly across
the room toward the bed, and, taking Gwen's
hand, he shook it up and down, and hurriedly said:

"Fine day, ma'am; hope I see you quite well."

"No; you don't," cried Gwen, laughing
immoderately, but keeping hold of Bill's hand, to
his great confusion. "I'm not well a bit, but I'm
a great deal better since hearing of your meeting,
Bill."

To this Bill made no reply, being entirely
engrossed in getting his hard, bony, brown hand
out of the grasp of the white, clinging fingers.

"Oh, Bill," went on Gwen, "it was delightful!
How did you do it?"

But Bill, who had by this time got back to his
seat at the door, pretended ignorance of any
achievement calling for remark. He "hadn't
done nothin' more out ov the way than usual."

"Oh, don't talk nonsense!" cried Gwen, impatiently. "Tell me how you got Scottie to lay you two hundred and fifty dollars."

"Oh, that!" said Bill, in great surprise; "that ain't nuthin' much. Scottie riz slick enough."

"But how did you get him?" persisted Gwen. "Tell me, Bill," she added, in her most coaxing voice.

"Well," said Bill, "it was easy as rollin' off a log. I made the remark as how the boys giner-ally put up for what they wanted without no fuss, and that if they was sot on havin' a Gospel shack I cherished the opinion"—here Gwen went off into a smothered shriek, which made Bill pause and look at her in alarm.

"Go on," she gasped.

"I cherished the opinion," drawled on Bill, while Gwen stuck her handkerchief into her mouth, "that mebbe they'd put up for it the seven hundred dollars, and, even as it was, seein' as The Pilot appeared to be sot on to it, if them fellers would find two hundred and fifty I cher——" another shriek from Gwen cut him suddenly short.

"It's the rheumaticks, mebbe," said Bill, anxic.sly. "Terrible bad weather for 'em. I get 'em myself."

"No, no," said Gwen, wiping away her tears and subduing her laughter. "Go on, Bill."

"There ain't no more," said Bill. "He bit, and the master here put it down."

"Yes, it's here right enough," I said, "but I don't suppose you mean to follow it up, do you?"

"You don't, eh? Well, I am not responsible for your supposin', but them that is familiar with Bronco Bill generally expects him to back up his undertakin's."

"But how in the world can you get five hundred dollars from the cowboys for a church?"

"I hain't done the arithmetic yet, but it's safe enough. You see, it ain't the church altogether, it's the reputation of the boys."

"I'll help, Bill," said Gwen.

Bill nodded his head slowly and said: "Proud to have you," trying hard to look enthusiastic.

"You don't think I can," said Gwen. Bill protested against such an imputation. "But I can. I'll get daddy and The Duke, too."

"Good line!" said Bill, slapping his knee.

"And I'll give all my money, too, but it isn't very much," she added, sadly.

"Much!" said Bill, "if the rest of the fellows

play up to that lead there won't be any trouble about that five hundred."

Gwen was silent for some time, then said with an air of resolve:

"I'll give my pinto!"

"Nonsense!" I exclaimed, while Bill declared "there warn't no call."

"Yes. I'll give the Pinto!" said Gwen, decidedly. "I'll not need him any more," her lips quivered, and Bill coughed and spat into the next room, "and besides, I want to give something I like. And Bill will sell him for me!"

"Well," said Bill, slowly, "now come to think, it'll be purty hard to sell that there pinto." Gwen began to exclaim indignantly, and Bill hurried on to say, "Not but what he ain't a good leetle horse for his weight, good leetle horse, but for cattle——"

"Why, Bill, there isn't a better cattle horse anywhere!"

"Yes, that's so," assented Bill. "That's so, if you've got the rider, but put one of them rangers on to him and it wouldn't be no fair show." Bill was growing more convinced every moment that the pinto wouldn't sell to any advantage. "Ye see," he explained carefully and cunningly, he ain't a horse you could yank round and slam into a bunch of steers regardless."

Gwen shuddered. "Oh, I wouldn't think of selling him to any of those cowboys." Bill crossed his legs and hitched round uncomfortably on his bench. "I mean one of those rough fellows that don't know how to treat a horse." Bill nodded, looking relieved. "I thought that some one like you, Bill, who knew how to handle a horse——"

Gwen paused, and then added: "I'll ask The Duke."

"No call for that," said Bill, hastily, "not but what The Dook ain't all right as a jedge of a horse, but The Dook ain't got the connection, it ain't his line." Bill hesitated. "But, if you are real sot on to sellin' that pinto, come to think I guess I could find a sale for him, though, of course, I think perhaps the figger won't be high."

And so it was arranged that the pinto should be sold and that Bill should have the selling of it.

It was characteristic of Gwen that she would not take farewell of the pony on whose back she had spent so many hours of freedom and delight. When once she gave him up she refused to allow her heart to cling to him any more.

It was characteristic, too, of Bill that he led off the pinto after night had fallen, so that "his pardner" might be saved the pain of the parting.

"This here's rather a new game for me, but when my pardner," here he jerked his head towards Gwen's window, "calls for trumps, I'm blanked if I don't throw my highest, if it costs a leg."

Bill's Financing

CHAPTER XVI

Bill's method of conducting the sale of the pinto was eminently successful as a financial operation, but there are those in the Swan Creek country who have never been able to fathom the mystery attaching to the affair. It was at the fall round-up, the beef round-up, as it is called, which this year ended at the Ashley Ranch. There were representatives from all the ranches and some cattle-men from across the line. The hospitality of the Ashley Ranch was up to its own lofty standard, and, after supper, the men were in a state of high exhilaration. The Hon. Fred and his wife, Lady Charlotte, gave themselves to the duties of their position as hosts for the day with a heartiness and grace beyond praise. After supper the men gathered round the big fire, which was piled up before the long, low shed, which stood open in front. It was a scene of such wild and picturesque interest as can only be witnessed in the western ranching country. About the fire, most of them wearing "shaps" and all of them wide, hard-brimmed cowboy hats, the men grouped themselves, some reclining upon skins thrown upon the ground, some standing, some sitting, smoking, laughing, chatting, all in highest spirits and humor. They had just got through with their season of arduous and, at times, dangerous toil. Their minds were full of their long, hard rides, their wild and varying experiences with mad cattle and bucking broncos, their anxious watchings through hot nights, when a breath of wind or a coyote's howl might set the herd off in a frantic stampede, their wolf hunts and badger fights and all the marvellous adventures that fill up a cowboy's summer. Now these were all behind them. To-night they were free men and of independent means, for their season's pay was in their pockets. The day's excitement, too, was still in their blood, and they were ready for anything.

Bill, as king of the bronco-busters, moved about with the slow, careless indifference of a man sure of his position and sure of his ability to maintain it.

He spoke seldom and slowly, was not as ready-witted as his partner, Hi Kendal, but in act he was swift and sure, and "in trouble" he could be counted on.   He was, as they said, "a white man; white to the back," which was understood to sum up the true cattle man's virtues.

"Hello, Bill," said a friend, "where's Hi? Hain't seen him around!"

"Well, don't jest know.   He was going to bring up my pinto."

"Your pinto?   What pinto's that?   You hain't got no pinto!"

"Mebbe not," said Bill, slowly, "but I had the idee before you spoke that I had."

"That so?   Whar'd ye git him?   Good for cattle?"   The crowd began to gather.

Bill grew mysterious, and even more than usually reserved.

"Good fer cattle!   Well, I ain't much on gamblin', but I've got a leetle in my pants that says that there pinto kin outwork any blanked bronco in this outfit, givin' him a fair show after the cattle."

The men became interested.

"Whar was he raised?"

"Dunno."

"Whar'd ye git him?   Across the line?"

"No," said Bill stoutly, "right in this here country.   The Dook there knows him."

This at once raised the pinto several points. To be known, and, as Bill's tone indicated, favorably known by The Duke, was a testimonial to which any horse might aspire.

"Whar'd ye git him, Bill?   Don't be so blanked oncommunicatin'!" said an impatient voice.

Bill hesitated; then, with an apparent burst of confidence, he assumed his frankest manner and voice, and told his tale.

"Well," he said, taking a fresh chew and offering his plug to his neighbor, who passed it on after helping himself, "ye see, it was like this. Ye know that little Meredith gel?"

Chorus of answers: "Yes!   The red-headed one. I know!   She's a daisy!—reg'lar blizzard!—lightnin' conductor!"

Bill paused, stiffened himself a little, dropped his frank air and drawled out in cool, hard tones: "I might remark that that young lady is, I might persoom to say, a friend of mine, which I'm prepared to back up in my best style, and if any blanked blanked son of a street sweeper has any remark to make, here's his time now!"

In the pause that followed murmurs were heard

extolling the many excellences of the young lady
in question, and Bill, appeased, yielded to the
requests for the continuance of his story, and, as
he described Gwen and her pinto and her work
on the ranch, the men, many of whom had had
glimpses of her, gave emphatic approval in their
own way. But as he told of her rescue of Joe and
of the sudden calamity that had befallen her a
great stillness fell upon the simple, tender-hearted
fellows, and they listened with their eyes shining
in the firelight with growing intentness. Then
Bill spoke of The Pilot and how he stood by her
and helped her and cheered her till they began to
swear he was "all right"; "and now," concluded
Bill, "when The Pilot is in a hole she wants to
help him out."

"O' course," said one. "Right enough.
How's she going to work it?" said another.

"Well, he's dead set on to buildin' a meetin'-
house, and them fellows down at the Creek that
does the prayin' and such don't seem to back him
up!"

"Whar's the kick, Bill?"

"Oh, they don't want to go down into their
clothes and put up for it."

"How much?"

"Why, he only asked 'em for seven hundred the hull outfit, and would give 'em two years, but they bucked—wouldn't look at it."

[Chorus of expletives descriptive of the characters and personal appearance and belongings of the congregation of Swan Creek.]

"Were you there, Bill? What did you do?"

"Oh," said Bill, modestly, "I didn't do much. Gave 'em a little bluff."

"No! How? What? Go on, Bill."

But Bill remained silent, till under strong pressure, and, as if making a clean breast of everything, he said:

"Well, I jest told 'em that if you boys made such a fuss about anythin' like they did about their Gospel outfit, an' I ain't sayin' anythin' agin it, you'd put up seven hundred without turnin' a hair."

"You're the stuff, Bill! Good man! You're talkin' now! What did they say to that, eh, Bill?"

"Well," said Bill, slowly, "they *called* me!"

"No! That so? An' what did you do, Bill?"

"Gave 'em a dead straight bluff!"

[Yells of enthusiastic approval.]

"Did they take you, Bill?"

"Well, I reckon they did. The master, here, put it down."

Whereupon I read the terms of Bill's bluff.

There was a chorus of very hearty approvals of Bill's course in "not taking any water" from that variously characterized "outfit." But the responsibility of the situation began to dawn upon them when some one asked:

"How are you going about it, Bill?"

"Well," drawled Bill, with a touch of sarcasm in his voice, "there's that pinto."

"Pinto be blanked!" said young Hill. "Say, boys, is that little girl going to lose that one pony of hers to help out her friend The Pilot? Good fellow, too, he is! We know he's the right sort."

[Chorus of, "Not by a long sight; not much; we'll put up the stuff! Pinto!"]

"Then," went on Bill, even more slowly, "there's The Pilot; he's going for to ante up a month's pay; 'taint much, o' course—twenty-eight a month and grub himself. He might make it two," he added, thoughtfully. But Bill's proposal was scorned with contemptuous groans. "Twenty-eight a month and grub himself o' course ain't much for a man to save money out ov to eddicate himself," Bill continued, as if thinking aloud, "O' course he's got his mother at home, but she can't make much more than her own livin', but she might help him some."

This was altogether too much for the crowd. They consigned Bill and his plans to unutterable depths of woe.

"O' course," Bill explained, "it's jest as you boys feel about it. Mebbe I was, bein' hot, a little swift in givin' 'em the bluff."

"Not much, you wasn't! We'll see you out! That's the talk! There's between twenty and thirty of us here."

"I should be glad to contribute thirty or forty if need be," said The Duke, who was standing not far off, "to assist in the building of a church. It would be a good thing, and I think the parson should be encouraged. He's the right sort."

"I'll cover your thirty," said young Hill; and so it went from one to another in tens and fifteens and twenties, till within half an hour I had entered three hundred and fifty dollars in my book, with Ashley yet to hear from, which meant fifty more. It was Bill's hour of triumph.

"Boys," he said, with solemn emphasis, "ye're all white. But that leetle pale-faced gel, that's what I'm thinkin' on. Won't she open them big eyes ov hers! I cherish the opinion that this'll tickle her some."

The men were greatly pleased with Bill and even more pleased with themselves. Bill's picture of the "leetle gel" and her pathetically tragic lot had gone right to their hearts and, with men of that stamp, it was one of their few luxuries to yield to their generous impulses. The most of them had few opportunities of lavishing love and sympathy upon worthy objects and, when the opportunity came, all that was best in them clamored for expression.

How the Pinto Sold

CHAPTER XVII

HOW THE PINTO SOLD

The glow of virtuous feeling following the performance of their generous act prepared the men for a keener enjoyment than usual of a night's sport. They had just begun to dispose themselves in groups about the fire for poker and other games when Hi rode up into the light and with him a stranger on Gwen's beautiful pinto pony.

Hi was evidently half drunk and, as he swung himself off his bronco, he saluted the company with a wave of the hand and hoped he saw them "kickin'."

Bill, looking curiously at Hi, went up to the pinto and, taking him by the head, led him up into the light, saying:

"See here, boys, there's that pinto of mine I was telling you about; no flies on him, eh?"

"Hold on there! Excuse me!" said the stranger, "this here hoss belongs to me, if paid-down money means anything in this country."

"The country's all right," said Bill in an ominously quiet voice, "but this here pinto's another transaction, I reckon."

"The hoss is mine, I say, and what's more, I'm goin' to hold him," said the stranger in a loud voice.

The men began to crowd around with faces growing hard. It was dangerous in that country to play fast and loose with horses.

"Look a-hyar, mates," said the stranger, with a Yankee drawl, "I ain't no hoss thief, and if I hain't bought this hoss reg'lar and paid down good money then it ain't mine—if I have it is. That's fair, ain't it?"

At this Hi pulled himself together, and in a half-drunken tone declared that the stranger was all right, and that he had bought the horse fair and square, and "there's your dust," said Hi, handing a roll to Bill. But with a quick movement Bill caught the stranger by the leg, and, before a word could be said, he was lying flat on the ground.

"You git off that pony," said Bill, "till this thing is settled."

There was something so terrible in Bill's manner that the man contented himself with blustering and swearing, while Bill, turning to Hi, said:

"Did you sell this pinto to him?"

Hi was able to acknowledge that, being offered a good price, and knowing that his partner was always ready for a deal, he had transferred the pinto to the stranger for forty dollars.

Bill was in distress, deep and poignant. " 'Taint the horse, but the leetle gel," he explained; but his partner's bargain was his, and wrathful as he was, he refused to attempt to break the bargain.

At this moment the Hon. Fred, noting the unusual excitement about the fire, came up, followed at a little distance by his wife and The Duke.

"Perhaps he'll sell," he suggested.

"No," said Bill sullenly, "he's a mean cuss."

"I know him," said the Hon. Fred, "let me try him." But the stranger declared the pinto suited him down to the ground and he wouldn't take twice his money for him.

"Why," he protested, "that there's what I call an unusual hoss, and down in Montana for a lady he'd fetch up to a hundred and fifty dollars." In vain they haggled and bargained; the man was immovable. Eighty dollars he wouldn't look at, a hundred hardly made him hesitate. At this point Lady Charlotte came down into the light and stood by her husband, who explained the circumstances to her. She had already heard Bill's description of Gwen's accident and of her part in the church-building schemes. There was silence for a few moments as she stood looking at the beautiful pony.

"What a shame the poor child should have to part with the dear little creature!" she said in a low tone to her husband. Then, turning to the stranger, she said in clear, sweet tones:

"What do you ask for him?" He hesitated and then said, lifting his hat awkwardly in salute: "I was just remarking how that pinto would fetch one hundred and fifty dollars down into Montana. But seein' as a lady is enquirin', I'll put him down to one hundred and twenty-five."

"Too much," she said promptly, "far too much, is it not, Bill?"

"Well," drawled Bill, "if 'twere a fellar as was used to ladies he'd offer you the pinto, but he's too pizen mean even to come down to the even hundred."

The Yankee took him up quickly. "Wall, if I were so blanked—pardon, madam"—taking off his hat, "used to ladies as some folks would like

to think themselves, I'd buy that there pinto and
make a present of it to this here lady as stands
before me." Bill twisted uneasily.

"But I ain't goin' to be mean; I'll put that
pinto in for the even money for the lady if any
man cares to put up the stuff."

"Well, my dear," said the Hon. Fred with a
bow, "we cannot well let that gage lie." She
turned and smiled at him and the pinto was
transferred to the Ashley stables, to Bill's out-
spoken delight, who declared he "couldn't have
faced the music if that there pinto had gone across
the line." I confess, however, I was somewhat
surprised at the ease with which Hi escaped his
wrath, and my surprise was in no way lessened
when I saw, later in the evening, the two partners
with the stranger taking a quiet drink out of the
same bottle with evident mutual admiration and
delight.

"You're an A1 corker, you are! I'll be
blanked if you ain't a bird—a singin' bird—a
reg'lar canary," I heard Hi say to Bill.

But Bill's only reply was a long, slow wink
which passed into a frown as he caught my eye.
My suspicion was aroused that the sale of the
pinto might bear investigation, and this suspicion

was deepened when Gwen next week gave me a rapturous account of how splendidly Bill had disposed of the pinto, showing me bills for one hundred and fifty dollars! To my look of amazement, Gwen replied:

"You see, he must have got them bidding against each other, and besides, Bill says pintos are going up."

Light began to dawn upon me, but I only answered that I knew they had risen very considerably in value within a month. The extra fifty was Bill's.

I was not present to witness the finishing of Bill's bluff, but was told that when Bill made his way through the crowded aisle and laid his five hundred and fifty dollars on the schoolhouse desk the look of disgust, surprise and finally of pleasure on Robbie's face, was worth a hundred more. But Robbie was ready and put down his two hundred with the single remark:

"Ay! ye're no as daft as ye look," mid roars of laughter from all.

Then The Pilot, with eyes and face shining, rose and thanked them all; but when he told of how the little girl in her lonely shack in the hills thought so much of the church that she gave up for it her beloved pony, her one possession, the light from his eyes glowed in the eyes of all.

But the men from the ranches who could understand the full meaning of her sacrifice and who also could realize the full measure of her calamity, were stirred to their hearts' depths, so that when Bill remarked in a very distinct undertone, "I cherish the opinion that this here Gospel shop wouldn't be materializin' into its present shape but for that leetle gel," there rose growls of approval in a variety of tones and expletives that left no doubt that his opinion was that of all.

But though The Pilot never could quite get at the true inwardness of Bill's measures and methods, and was doubtless all the more comfortable in mind for that, he had no doubt that while Gwen's influence was the moving spring of action, Bill's bluff had a good deal to do with the "materializin'" of the first church in Swan Creek, and in this conviction, I share.

Whether the Hon. Fred ever understood the peculiar style of Bill's financing, I do not quite know. But if he ever did come to know, he was far too much of a man to make a fuss. Besides, I fancy the smile on his lady's face was worth

some large amount to him.   At least, so the look
of proud and fond love in his eyes seemed to say
as he turned away with her from the fire the
night of the pinto's sale.

The Lady Charlotte

CHAPTER XVIII

THE LADY CHARLOTTE

The night of the pinto's sale was a night momentous to Gwen, for then it was that the Lady Charlotte's interest in her began. Momentous, too, to the Lady Charlotte, for it was that night that brought The Pilot into her life

I had turned back to the fire around which the men had fallen into groups prepared to have an hour's solid delight, for the scene was full of wild and picturesque beauty to me, when The Duke came and touched me on the shoulder.

"Lady Charlotte would like to see you."

"And why, pray?"

"She wants to hear about this affair of Bill's."

We went through the kitchen into the large dining-room, at one end of which was a stone chimney and fireplace. Lady Charlotte had declared that she did not much care what kind of a house the Hon. Fred would build for her, but that she must have a fireplace.

She was very beautiful—tall, slight and graceful in every line. There was a reserve and a grand air in her bearing that put people in awe of her. This awe I shared; but as I entered the room she welcomed me with such kindly grace that I felt quite at ease in a moment.

"Come and sit by me," she said, drawing an armchair into the circle about the fire. "I want you to tell us all about a great many things."

"You see what you're in for, Connor," said her husband. "It is a serious business when my lady takes one in hand."

"As he knows to his cost," she said, smiling and shaking her head at her husband.

"So I can testify," put in The Duke.

"Ah! I can't do anything with you," she replied, turning to him.

"Your most abject slave," he replied with a profound bow.

"If you only were," smiling at him—a little sadly, I thought—"I'd keep you out of all sorts of mischief."

"Quite true, Duke," said her husband, "just look at me."

The Duke gazed at him a moment or two. "Wonderful!" he murmured, "what a deliverance!"

"Nonsense!" broke in Lady Charlotte. "You are turning my mind away from my purpose."

"Is it possible, do you think?" said The Duke to her husband.

"Not in the very least," he replied, "if my experience goes for anything."

But Lady Charlotte turned her back upon them and said to me:

"Now, tell me first about Bill's encounter with that funny little Scotchman."

Then I told her the story of Bill's bluff in my best style, imitating, as I have some small skill in doing, the manner and speech of the various actors in the scene. She was greatly amused and interested.

"And Bill has really got his share ready," she cried. "It is very clever of him."

"Yes," I replied, "but Bill is only the very humble instrument, the moving spirit is behind."

"Oh, yes, you mean the little girl that owns the pony," she said. "That's another thing you must tell me about."

"The Duke knows more than I," I replied, shifting the burden to him; "my acquaintance is only of yesterday; his is lifelong."

"Why have you never told me of her?" she demanded, turning to the Duke.

"Haven't I told you of the little Meredith girl? Surely I have," said The Duke, hesitatingly.

"Now, you know quite well you have not, and that means you are deeply interested. Oh, I know you well," she said, severely.

"He is the most secretive man," she went on to me, "shamefully and ungratefully reserved."

The Duke smiled; then said, lazily: "Why, she's just a child. Why should you be interested in her? No one was," he added sadly, "till misfortune distinguished her."

Her eyes grew soft, and her gay manner changed, and she said to The Duke gently: "Tell me of her now."

It was evidently an effort, but he began his story of Gwen from the time he saw her first, years ago, playing in and out of her father's rambling shack, shy and wild as a young fox. As he went on with his tale, his voice dropped into a low, musical tone, and he seemed as if dreaming aloud. Unconsciously he put into the tale much of himself, revealing how great an influence the little child had had upon him, and how empty of love his life had been in this lonely land. Lady

Charlotte listened with face intent upon him, and even her bluff husband was conscious that something more than usual was happening. He had never heard The Duke break through his proud reserve before.

But when The Duke told the story of Gwen's awful fall, which he did with great graphic power, a little red spot burned upon the Lady Charlotte's pale cheek, and, as The Duke finished his tale with the words, "It was her last ride," she covered her face with her hands and cried:

"Oh, Duke, it is horrible to think of! But what splendid courage!"

"Great stuff! eh, Duke?" cried the Hon. Fred, kicking a burning log vigorously.

But The Duke made no reply.

"How is she now, Duke?" said Lady Charlotte.

The Duke looked up as from a dream. "Bright as the morning," he said. Then, in reply to Lady Charlotte's look of wonder, he added:

"The Pilot did it. Connor will tell you. I don't understand it."

"Nor do I, either. But I can tell you only what I saw and heard," I answered.

"Tell me," said Lady Charlotte very gently.

Then I told her how, one by one, we had failed

to help her, and how The Pilot had ridden up
that morning through the canyon, and how he
had brought the first light and peace to her by his
marvellous pictures of the flowers and ferns and
trees and all the wonderful mysteries of that wonderful canyon.

"But that wasn't all," said the Duke quickly,
as I stopped.

"No," I said slowly, "that was *not* all by a long
way; but the rest I don't understand. That's
The Pilot's secret."

"Tell me what he did," said Lady Charlotte,
softly, once more. "I want to know."

"I don't think I can," I replied. "He simply
read out of the Scriptures to her and talked."

Lady Charlotte looked disappointed.

"Is that all?" she said.

"It is quite enough for Gwen," said The Duke
confidently, "for there she lies, often suffering,
always longing for the hills and the free air, but
with her face radiant as the flowers of the beloved
canyon."

"I must see her," said Lady Charlotte, "and
that wonderful Pilot."

"You'll be disappointed in him," said The
Duke.

"Oh, I've see him and heard him, but I don't know him," she replied. "There must be something in him that one does not see at first."

"So I have discovered," said The Duke, and with that the subject was dropped, but not before the Lady Charlotte made me promise to take her to Gwen, The Duke being strangely unwilling to do this for her.

"You'll be disappointed," he said. "She is only a simple little child."

But Lady Charlotte thought differently, and, having made up her mind upon the matter, there was nothing for it, as her husband said, but "for all hands to surrender and the sooner the better."

And so the Lady Charlotte had her way, which, as it turned out, was much the wisest and best.

Through Gwen's Window

CHAPTER XIX

When I told The Pilot of Lady Charlotte's purpose to visit Gwen, he was not too well pleased.

"What does she want with Gwen?" he said impatiently. "She will just put notions into her head and make the child discontented."

"Why should she?" said I.

"She won't mean to, but she belongs to another world, and Gwen cannot talk to her without getting glimpses of a life that will make her long for what she can never have," said The Pilot.

"But suppose it is not idle curiosity in Lady Charlotte," I suggested.

"I don't say it is quite that," he answered, "but these people love a sensation."

"I don't think you know Lady Charlotte," I replied. "I hardly think from her tone the other night that she is a sensation hunter."

"At any rate," he answered, decidedly, "she is not to worry poor Gwen."

241

I was a little surprised at his attitude, and felt that he was unfair to Lady Charlotte, but I forbore to argue with him on the matter. He could not bear to think of any person or thing threatening the peace of his beloved Gwen.

The very first Saturday after my promise was given we were surprised to see Lady Charlotte ride up to the door of our shack in the early morning.

"You see, I am not going to let you off," she said, as I greeted her. "And the day is so very fine for a ride."

I hastened to apologize for not going to her, and then to get out of my difficulty, rather meanly turned toward The Pilot, and said:

"The Pilot doesn't approve of our visit."

"And why not, may I ask?" said Lady Charlotte, lifting her eyebrows.

The Pilot's face burned, partly with wrath at me, and partly with embarrassment; for Lady Charlotte had put on her grand air. But he stood to his guns.

"I was saying, Lady Charlotte," he said, looking straight into her eyes, "that you and Gwen have little in common—and—and—" he hesitated.

"Little in common!" said Lady Charlotte quietly. "She has suffered greatly."

The Pilot was quick to catch the note of sadness in her voice.

"Yes," he said, wondering at her tone, "she has suffered greatly."

"And," continued Lady Charlotte, "she is bright as the morning, The Duke says." There was a look of pain in her face.

The Pilot's face lit up, and he came nearer and laid his hand caressingly upon her beautiful horse.

"Yes, thank God!" he said quickly, "bright as the morning."

"How can that be?" she asked, looking down into his face. "Perhaps she would tell me."

"Lady Charlotte," said The Pilot with a sudden flush, "I must ask your pardon. I was wrong. I thought you—" he paused; "but go to Gwen, she will tell you, and you will do her good."

"Thank you," said Lady Charlotte, putting out her hand, "and perhaps you will come and see me, too."

The Pilot promised and stood looking after us as we rode up the trail.

"There is something more in your Pilot than at

first appears," she said. "The Duke was quite right."

"He is a great man," I said with enthusiasm; "tender as a woman and with the heart of a hero."

"You and Bill and The Duke seem to agree about him," she said, smiling.

Then I told her tales of The Pilot, and of his ways with the men, till her blue eyes grew bright and her beautiful face lost its proud look.

"It is perfectly amazing," I said, finishing my story, "how these devil-may-care rough fellows respect him, and come to him in all sorts of trouble. I can't understand it, and yet he is just a boy."

"No, not amazing," said Lady Charlotte slowly. "I think I understand it. He has a true man's heart, and holds a great purpose in it. I've seen men like that. Not clergymen, I mean, but men with a great purpose."

Then, after a moment's thought, she added: "But you ought to care for him better. He does not look strong."

"Strong!" I exclaimed quickly, with a queer feeling of resentment at my heart. "He can do as much riding as any of us."

"Still," she replied, "there's something in his face that would make his mother anxious." In spite of my repudiation of her suggestion, I found myself for the next few minutes thinking of how he would come exhausted and faint from his long rides, and I resolved that he must have a rest and change.

It was one of those early September days, the best of all in the western country, when the light falls less fiercely through a soft haze that seems to fill the air about you, and that grows into purple on the far hilltops.   By the time we reached the canyon the sun was riding high and pouring its rays full into all the deep nooks where the shadows mostly lay.

There were no shadows to-day, except such as the trees cast upon the green moss beds and the black rocks.   The tops of the tall elms were sere and rusty, but the leaves of the rugged oaks that fringed the canyon's lips shone a rich and glossy brown.   All down the sides the poplars and delicate birches, pale yellow, but sometimes flushing into orange and red, stood shimmering in the golden light, while here and there the broad-spreading, feathery sumachs made great splashes of brilliant crimson upon the yellow and gold.

said Bill, with careful indifference, but he added to himself, "except his, of course."

"Come in, Bill," I urged. "It will look queer, you know," but Bill replied:

"I guess I'll not bother," adding, after a pause: "You see, there's them wimmin turnin' on the waterworks, and like as not they'd swamp me sure."

"That's so," said Hi, who was standing near, in silent sympathy with his friend's grief.

I reported to Gwen, who answered in her old imperious way, "Tell him I want him." I took Bill the message.

"Why didn't you say so before?" he said, and, starting up, he passed into the house and took up his position behind Gwen's chair. Opposite, and leaning against the door, stood The Duke, with a look of quiet earnestness on his handsome face. At his side stood the Hon. Fred Ashley, and behind him the Old Timer, looking bewildered and woe-stricken. The Pilot had filled a large place in the old man's life. The rest of the men stood about the room and filled the kitchen beyond, all quiet, solemn, sad.

In Gwen's room, the one farthest in, lay The Pilot, stately and beautiful under the magic touch of death. And as I stood and looked down upon the quiet face I saw why Gwen shed no tear, but carried a look of serene triumph. She had read the face aright. The lines of weariness that had been growing so painfully clear the last few months were smoothed out, the look of care was gone, and in place of weariness and care was the proud smile of victory and peace. He had met his foe and was surprised to find his terror gone.

The service was beautiful in its simplicity. The minister, The Pilot's chief, had come out from town to take charge. He was rather a little man, but sturdy and well set. His face was burnt and seared with the suns and frosts he had braved for years. Still in the prime of his manhood, his hair and beard were grizzled and his face deep-lined, for the toils and cares of a pioneer mission-ary's life are neither few nor light. But out of his kindly blue eye looked the heart of a hero, and as he spoke to us we felt the prophet's touch and caught a gleam of the prophet's fire.

"I have fought the fight," he read. The ring in his voice lifted up all our heads, and, as he pictured to us the life of that battered hero who had written these words, I saw Bill's eyes begin to gleam and his lank figure straighten out its

lazy angles.   Then he turned the leaves quickly
and read again, "Let not your heart be troubled
. . . in my father's house are many mansions."
His voice took a lower, sweeter tone; he looked
over our heads, and for a few moments spoke of
the eternal hope.   Then he came back to us, and,
looking round into the faces turned so eagerly to
him, talked to us of The Pilot—how at the first he
had sent him to us with fear and trembling—he
was so young—but how he had come to trust in
him and to rejoice in his work, and to hope much
from his life.   Now it was all over; but he felt
sure his young friend had not given his life in
vain.   He paused as he looked from one to the
other, till his eyes rested on Gwen's face.   I was
startled, as I believe he was, too, at the smile that
parted her lips, so evidently saying: "Yes, but
how much better I know than you."

"Yes," ne went on, after a pause, answering
her smile, "you all know better than I that his
work among you will not pass away with his
removal, but endure while you live," and the
smile on Gwen's face grew brighter.   "And now
you must not grudge him his reward and his rest
. . . and his home."   And Bill, nodding his head
slowly, said under his breath, "That's so."

Then they sang that hymn of the dawning
glory of Immanuel's land,—Lady Charlotte playing the organ and The Duke leading with clear,
steady voice verse after verse. When they came
to the last verse the minister made a sign and,
while they waited, he read the words:

> "I've wrestled on towards heaven
>   'Gainst storm, and wind, and tide."

And so on to that last victorious cry,—

> "I hail the glory dawning
>   In Immanuel's Land."

For a moment it looked as if the singing could
not go on, for tears were on the minister's face
and the women were beginning to sob, but The
Duke's clear, quiet voice caught up the song and
steadied them all to the end.

After the prayer, they all went in and looked at
The Pilot's face and passed out, leaving behind
only those that knew him best. The Duke and
the Hon. Fred stood looking down upon the quiet
face.

"The country has lost a good man, Duke," said

the Hon. Fred.   The Duke bowed silently.   Then
Lady Charlotte came and gazed a moment.

"Dear Pilot," she whispered, her tears falling
fast. "Dear, dear Pilot! Thank God for you!
You have done much for me." Then she stooped
and kissed him on his cold lips and on his forehead.

Then Gwen seemed to suddenly waken as from
a dream.   She turned and, looking up in a fright-
ened way, said to Bill hurriedly:

"I want to see him again.   Carry me!"

And Bill gathered her up in his arms and took
her in.   As they looked down upon the dead face
with its look of proud peace and touched with the
stateliness of death, Gwen's fear passed away,
But when The Duke made to cover the face.
Gwen drew a sharp breath and, clinging to Bill,
said, with a sudden gasp:

"Oh, Bill, I can't bear it alone.   I'm afraid
alone."

She was thinking of the long, weary days of
pain before her that she must face now without
The Pilot's touch and smile and voice.

"Me, too," said Bill, thinking of the days
before him.   He could have said nothing better.
Gwen looked in his face a moment, then said:

"We'll help each other," and Bill, swallowing hard, could only nod his head in reply. Once more they looked upon The Pilot, leaning down and lingering over him, and then Gwen said quietly:

"Take me away, Bill," and Bill carried her into the outer room. Turning back I caught a look on The Duke's face so full of grief that I could not help showing my amazement. He noticed and said:

"The best man I ever knew, Connor. He has done something for me too. . . . I'd give the world to die like that."

Then he covered the face.

We sat at Gwen's window, Bill, with Gwen in his arms, and I watching. Down the sloping, snow-covered hill wound the procession of sleighs and horsemen, without sound of voice or jingle of bell till, one by one, they passed out of our sight and dipped down into the canyon. But we knew every step of the winding trail and followed them in fancy through that fairy scene of mystic wonderland. We knew how the great elms and the poplars and the birches clinging to the snowy sides interlaced their bare boughs into a network of bewildering complexity, and how the cedars

and balsams and spruces stood in the bottom,
their dark boughs weighted down with heavy
white mantles of snow, and how every stump
and fallen log and rotting stick was made a thing
of beauty by the snow that had fallen so gently
on them in that quiet spot.   And we could see
the rocks of the canyon sides gleam out black
from under overhanging snow-banks, and we
could hear the song of the Swan in its many
tones, now under an icy sheet, cooing comfortably,
and then bursting out into sunlit laughter and
leaping into a foaming pool, to glide away
smoothly murmuring its delight to the white
banks that curved to kiss the dark water as it
fled.   And where the flowers had been, the
violets and the wind-flowers and the clematis and
the columbine and all the ferns and flowering
shrubs, there lay the snow.   Everywhere the
snow, pure, white, and myriad-gemmed, but
every flake a flower's shroud.

Out where the canyon opened to the sunny,
sloping prairie, there they would lay The Pilot
to sleep, within touch of the canyon he loved,
with all its sleeping things.   And there he lies to
this time.   But Spring has come many times to
the canyon since that winter day, and has called

to the sleeping flowers, summoning them forth in merry troops, and ever more and more till the canyon ripples with them. And lives are like flowers. In dying they abide not alone, but sow themselves and bloom again with each returning spring, and ever more and more.

For often during the following years, as here and there I came upon one of those that companied with us in those Foothill days, I would catch a glimpse in word and deed and look of him we called, first in jest, but afterwards with true and tender feeling we were not ashamed to own our Sky Pilot.

THE END